CONFLICT
MANAGEMENT

The Courage
To Confront

Richard J. Mayer

BATTELLE PRESS
Columbus • Richland

HD
42
M39
1990

Library of Congress Cataloging-in-Publication Data:

Mayer, Richard J., 1931–
        Conflict management: The courage to confront/Richard J. Mayer.
            p.   cm.
        Includes bibliographical references.
        ISBN 0–935470–51–4: $24.50
            1. Conflict management.   2. Organizational effectiveness.
        3. Organizational behavior.   4. Title.
        HD42.M39   1989
        658.4—dc20

89–38236
CIP

Additional copies may be ordered through Battelle Press, 505 King Avenue, Columbus, Ohio 43201, U.S.A., (614) 424-6393, or 1-800-451-3543.

ACKNOWLEDGEMENTS

Years ago, during a glimpse of all that life had given me, I walked the beach at sunset with a glowing sense of heartfelt gratitude for all my teachers. I found myself attempting to silently thank every person I had ever met. Such is the case with this book. It owes its existence to the countless people I've worked with in their courageous struggles for conflict resolution, effective leadership, self improvement, successful relationships, and organizations that work. Helping them helped me. I'd like to thank them all.

Perhaps even more, it springs from the hearts of those who helped directly to prepare me for the unusual professional role I've filled for the past two decades. Among them are: my wonderful family—Marlys, Michael, Paul, and Rich; my extraordinary mentors—David Freeman, Ph.D., Karl Humiston, M.D., Baba Muktananda, Siddha Meditation Master, Ansel Cobb, body-fender repairman, and Jim Good, friend; and the writings of countless sages, saints, psychologists, and authors.

My special thanks to Barbara Hoven, secretary extraordinaire, who typed the manuscript, helped edit it, and provided strong support during the many revisions. And to Jodi Smith, who typed the final draft.

I also want to express my gratitude to Cher Paul: her alert and sensitive editing put the polish on the manuscript before it went to press.

To the management and staff of Battelle with whom I've had the privilege of working during most of my years as a conflict management facilitator and teacher, I offer my deepest appreciation.

Leila Counts and Evelyn Kennedy did much to bring my first book (unpublished) into being, from which some of this material was taken. My thanks to them.

Also, my warmest thanks to my colleagues and group participants in the U.C.L.A. Leadership and Human Relations Laboratories, and to those who have attended my Insight Workshops. We have shared some of the gentle and amazing benefits of caring confrontation.

A Special Acknowledgment

Dr. William A. Hitt deserves a very special acknowledgment. Bill, a noted author (*The Leader-Manager: Guidelines for Action* and *Management in Action: Guidelines for New Managers,* both from Battelle Press) and teacher of management and leadership, calls this "a book of gems." He deserves much of the credit. Bill's ideas resulted in the title and the basic format. He also graciously and generously supplied most of the quotes in windows from his personal collection gathered over three decades of study.

He has been a good friend and a wonderfully supportive colleague whose encouragement and contributions made all the difference.

How to Read This Book

This book attempts to present glimpses of the wisdom expressed through the ages on managing conflict, the primary mechanics and how-to's of conflict management, and some of the special insights derived from the author's two decades of work as a facilitator with individuals and groups in conflict.

The first, the accumulated wisdom of centuries, is represented in part by quotations. Some are presented in the text. But because presenting too many in this way would disrupt the flow for the reader, a group constituting a marvelous view of the subject in itself is set off in occasional "windows" at the tops of pages throughout the book.

You may choose to read this sequence of quotations before reading the text to sense the spirit of the subject as elucidated by many inspired authors. Or they can be ignored at first and read later as support, confirmation, and illumination of the material.

Enjoy.

CONTENTS

PREFACE

During the past two decades, as a personal and organizational development consultant and trainer, I have taught, counseled, facilitated, and spoken on many subjects related to people and organizations. By far the most requested subject has been conflict management. This is not surprising since the management of conflict is a key to all relationships—to the effectiveness of individuals, couples, groups, and organizations.

Skillful conflict management can turn many of life's most disagreeable experiences into avenues for growth and self-realization. Conflict can be a gift that helps us attain our potential.

Over the years, many people have asked me for references on the subject of conflict management—something they can read, relate to, and put to use in their lives. I have not found a reference that deals to my satisfaction with the skills required to confront both ourselves and others. These two skills must be combined if we are to be successful in finding lasting resolutions and freeing ourselves from destructive conflicts. That is what this book is about.

The first part of the book lays out some simple conflict resolution skills that I've been teaching for almost a quarter century. The second part of the book derives from a workshop I've led for ten years called "Insight." The material from this workshop has helped hundreds of people resolve both personal and organizational conflicts.

I wish I could acknowledge all those who have taught me the skills covered in this book, but the years have been too many and the number too great. Ultimately, I have learned most from those I have taught and assisted in their struggles to resolve and avert destructive conflicts, to grow as individuals, and to improve their organizations. I sincerely hope this book acts to increase your courage and ability to confront, and that it helps you find the freedom and fulfillment that can result from effective confrontation.

Dick Mayer

CONFLICT MANAGEMENT

The Courage
To Confront

I
P A R T

THE NATURE OF CONFLICT

The Dilemma

*No two people think alike on everything.
No two people feel the same way at
all times within a relationship.
No two people want the same things
or want them at the same time.
People operate from different time tables.
We are, in fact, autonomous, different,
and unique beings.
Yet we are, at the same time, dependent
on others. We need them to help us get
many of the things we want (or not
prevent us from getting them). We are
also dependent on others to validate our
existence and worth.*

Virginia Satir [51]

Conflict can be a source of joy or pain, a benefit or burden, a blessing or curse, a gift or a torment, depending on how it is handled. Too often, the unique opportunities inherent in conflict situations are missed and the worst allowed to happen unnecessarily. Part I introduces the subject of how to manage conflict to profit from it. The skills required are simple. They begin with the understanding of how most destructive interpersonal conflicts develop and the essential elements of face-to-face communication.

A Part of Life

Conflict is a part of life, at least as we know it. How we deal with the fact of conflict has much to do with how we express our being.

J.F.T. Bugental[8]

CONFLICT

I've had a few arguments with people, but I never carry a grudge. You know why? While you're carrying a grudge, they're out dancing.

Buddy Hackett

Conflict has a bad name. People associate it with destructive-ness—with antagonism, uncomfortable relationships, loss of jobs, broken families, violence, and war. This understandable human reaction leads to the avoidance of confrontation, which paradoxically, is a primary reason conflicts grow to destructive proportions. This reaction also obscures the necessity of managing, rather than avoiding, conflict to the success of any organization. The full success of commercial organizations, government groups, families, and friendships depends upon the willingness to address differences and the know-how to do so effectively.

Conflict is threatening, yet it is inevitable in vital relationships. Managing conflict so that we may enjoy its benefits and prevent its potential destructiveness requires courage. The courage required diminishes as we develop the skills to confront effectively. The threat fades as we experience the salutary influence skillful confrontation has on our relationships and on our effectiveness. It often takes so little to prevent difficulties arising from differences that, once we learn how, we wonder why we haven't been doing so all our lives.

Managing conflict often requires confronting others. Part II of this book describes the attitudes and simple skills that can enable us to do so in positive and potent ways. The benefits resulting from their application will be evident almost immediately: precluding, alleviating, remediating, and resolving destructive conflicts. They also bring us new levels of intimacy, greater credibility, superior decisions, enhanced creativity, heightened mutual trust, improved teamwork, increased productivity, and more fun.

> *Opposition brings concord. Out of*
> *discord comes the fairest harmony.*
> *Heraclitus (c. 500 B.C.)*

To confront others capably, we must deal with ourselves. Part III discusses the benefits of, and the proven methods for, self-confrontation. Confronting others and confronting ourselves can work in concert to push us toward the realization of our full potential as human beings. Those who differ with us can stimulate our growth. We can learn to be grateful for, rather than upset with, the disagreements life inevitably presents to us.

We eliminate the destructive conflicts in our lives as we come to understand that their true origins are most often within us. Self-discovery, too, requires courage, and this courage gives way to confidence as we experience the freedom, peace, and competence truth brings to us.

> *We find comfort among those who agree*
> *with us—growth among those who don't.*
> *Frank A. Clark*

The skills of conflict management and self-discovery are simple, but not necessarily easy. They must be practiced to bear fruit. The reader is urged not to stop with the intellectual satisfaction of reading this book, but to proceed with practice. A lifetime of practice will help bring a lifetime of improvement. Please don't be disheartened when, with the best of intentions, you do your utmost without success. Human systems have no panaceas; nothing always works with everyone.[37]

As the song says, just pick yourself up, dust yourself off, and start all over again. You won't fail in the long run.

> *You're going to spend the rest of your*
> *life getting up one more time when*
> *you're knocked down—so you'd better*
> *start getting used to it.*
> *John Wayne*
> *(The Train Robbers, 1972)*

Moral: Conflict can bring the best or the worst life has to offer. Learn to avail yourself of its benefits and to minimize its drawbacks.

Toward a Greater Depth of Living

But we cannot avoid *conflict*, conflict with society, other individuals and with oneself. Conflicts may be sources of defeat, lost life and a limitation of our potentiality, but they may also lead to a greater depth of living and the birth of more far-reaching unities, which flourish in the tensions that engender them.

Karl Jaspers[19]

PREDICTABLE FACTORS MARKING CONFLICTS

Let us not be afraid of debate or dissent—let us encourage it. For if we should ever abandon these basic American traditions in the name of fighting Communism, what would it profit us to win the world when we have lost our soul?

John F. Kennedy

During the past 20 years, I have worked as a third party facilitator in over 2,000 interpersonal and group conflict situations, primarily in organizational settings (research and development organizations, engineering companies, hospitals, churches, youth organizations, a mental health center). Prior to that time, I was a line manager. I believe we should be aware of a number of factors if we are to use conflict constructively and to preclude and/or manage its destructive aspects. Some of these factors are virtually predictable:

1. When significant conflicts arise, each person involved typically believes he or she knows its cause (usually centered on the other person or persons).

2. Actually, the protagonists in a conflict almost *never* know its cause; their diagnoses are almost *always* in error. More often than not, the cause they ascribe has little or no bearing on the conflict.

3. Conflicts perceived to be rooted in action and content are in reality often caused by communication failures, particularly in listening.

4. In spite of beliefs to the contrary, deliberate workplace attempts by one person to harm another in any way are extremely rare.

5. The *need to be right*—a strong drive in most of us—is, almost invariably, a primary contributor to any conflict.

6. Many conflicts are fed by our belief in the primacy of rational thinking and a one-to-one correspondence between words (especially written words) and their meanings. We tend not to recognize that everyone interprets reality subjectively and that the meanings of most words are rooted in individual experience. This leads to overreliance on words and insensitivity to nonverbal communication.

7. By the time a conflict has attained the proportions most people are willing to—or feel they have to—deal with, the apparent conflict is actually an accumulation of numerous half-forgotten, relatively minor incidents leading to a blowup over the last straw. Because of this underlying complexity, often coupled with faulty communication patterns, third party assistance may be required for resolution.

8. Most interpersonal conflicts involve a dance—a series of moves and countermoves by each of the protagonists—with *no one to blame.*

Consider the following real-life example as illustrative of some of these factors.

Not long ago, two managers came to me, one at a time, to seek help for their five-year-old conflict. They had temporarily been able to put the conflict behind them because a company reorganization had separated them. However, a subsequent reorganization put them back into interdependent roles. They still could not get along and decided to seek my assistance.

I heard each of their stories. Each blamed the other for the problem and listed many justifying reasons. As usual, each story was impeccably logical and made perfect sense, the two stories were almost diametrically opposed, and I couldn't find a loophole in either. They agreed to meet for a conflict resolution session with me as the third party facilitator.

We met in a conference room at 8:00 A.M. We first went through a process of posting all the grievances on sheets of newsprint so they were visible to all of us. We next set priorities. Then I asked them to work on their issues in priority order. They did so, and as they proceeded I was able to observe the following pattern of communication: She would explain her viewpoint on an issue; when she finished her explanation, his response was to simply sit and look at her with no comment; she (assuming his apparent lack of response meant he didn't understand) repeated her views from a different angle; again, his response was a silent look; she would again repeat, varying her approach; he remained silent.

During his private meeting with me prior to our mutual session, he had complained about her talking too much and repeating her explanations *ad nauseam*. She had complained about him discounting and belittling her views, his lack of listening to her, and the tremendous effort required to communicate with him. It never occurred to him to stop their dance by letting her know—perhaps by saying something in response—that he heard what she said. His personal style was simply to listen without response if he had no questions! Likewise, she didn't think of ending their dance by stopping at the conclusion of an input or explanation and asking him for some response. Her style was to assume that his silence indicated indifference, disapproval, or lack of understanding and to keep on trying!

Either could easily have ended the destructive pattern of communication. They each simply lacked awareness of what was going on. Neither was to blame, as the other believed; neither was at fault, as the other thought; none of the motives each attributed to the other was accurate; neither explanation of the problem between them was even partially correct. The five-year accumulation of apparent problems and the bitter conflict between them was entirely due to their pattern of communication. Becoming aware of their dance ended their conflict and turned their relationship around. Knowing the truth set them free, as so often is the case.

> Moral: When you find yourself involved
> in a well-established, destructive
> conflict, don't assume that you
> know its cause, that anyone is
> to blame, or that the other
> person is deliberately attempting
> to hurt you. Dedicate yourself to
> the discovery of what's truly
> going on before taking any
> action. The situation may call
> for third party assistance.

Growth in Personality

Growth in personality occurs as a consequence of meeting conflicts and impasses head on, and reconciling them. Interpersonal conflicts and impasses constitute problems which require solution so that a satisfying relationship may be maintained. Whenever a person encounters a problem in his everyday living, he is obliged to vary his behavior until he discovers some mode of responding which is successful in achieving a solution.

Sidney Jourard[23]

COMMUNICATION, THE ALMOST IMPOSSIBLE DREAM

From listening comes wisdom, and from speaking repentance.

Italian Proverb

Before we get into the management of conflict, it will help us to consider the communication process itself. A highly useful and practical attitude is to assume interpersonal communication is almost *impossible* and thus requires lots of hard work. We will consider this from a fairly fundamental viewpoint in Part III.

For now, look at Figure 1. This simple figure presents a partial picture of the complexity of the communication process between just two individuals. (The complexity multiplies enormously in group settings.)

The Secret Code

We actually communicate in secret codes made up of words, non-verbal signals, "vibes"—maybe even E.S.P.—that are augmented and distorted by thoughts and feelings. With the help of Figure 1, let's explore an apparently simple, single-sentence communication as an example.

Suppose Maria turns to Jill and says, "Do you enjoy teamwork?" Consider first the environment in which this conversation takes place. Maria, who is thinking and feeling something, formulates the sentence and voices it while looking directly at Jill. Electromagnetic radiation, which we call "light," is bouncing off of Jill and the surroundings and registering on Maria via her visual senses. The sound waves emanating from Maria's mouth carry the sentence to both their ears and thereby affect both of them. Light bouncing off Maria and the surroundings is sensed by Jill. Maria is also sending a rich and complex nonverbal message consisting of her voice tone, appearance, body stance, vibes, and who knows what else. Each is reacting to this environment—the temperature, scenery, decor, location, and so forth. In addition, each is being influenced by her own outlook at this particular moment—an outlook influenced by personality factors, life history, other concurrent events, mood, physical condition, desires, thoughts, feelings, and other stored information such as stereotypes.

The communication that actually takes place when Maria says "Do you enjoy teamwork?" depends on all of these factors, plus. Suppose, for example, that Maria is Jill's boss and is upset with her for not being a team player. The question in that case is actually a statement to the

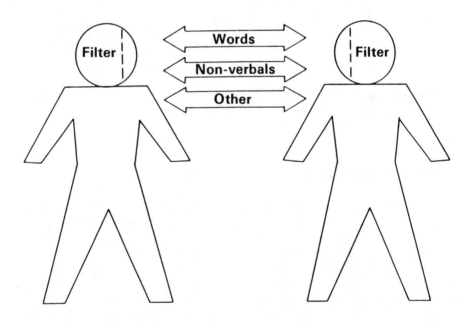

Figure 1. Communicating

effect that Jill does not perform to expectations. Jill may or may not hear the statement, depending upon Maria's nonverbal communications. If Maria is obviously angry, perhaps with a stern facial expression, a rasping voice tone, and clenched fists, Jill may hear, "You're in trouble!" She may or may not know what kind of trouble since the word "teamwork" has so many definitions and can conjure up so many images depending upon life experience. Maria, as is so often the case, may believe that her meaning of the word is accurate and precise so that Jill could not possibly miss hearing the message accurately. (A "team" to some people is a group wherein the members must relinquish their individuality; to others, the word has virtually the opposite meaning, and many definitions are possible between those extremes.) If Jill feels that she is an obvious and ardent team player, Maria's real message may be missed; it may even be heard as a joke or compliment.

Imagine another scenario. Let's say Maria is Jill's boss and is contemplating moving her from an individual contributor role where she is performing superlatively to a position on a highly interdependent team. Because Maria thinks highly of Jill and wants to keep her happy, she asks the question of Jill before making the decision. Maria asks the question as a question, exhibiting great warmth and respect toward Jill. Jill may hear a very different message if, say, she feels inadequate about her ability to work as a member of a team: she might have been criticized by someone else in the past for poor teamwork. Jill may even hear the message as criticism and become hostile and defensive. Chances are that she would misinterpret the message if her son had just been kicked off the Little League team, if her spouse had just left her, if she had run over the cat that morning, or if she was otherwise preoccupied.

Maybe Jill believes that Maria is obviously not a team player, thus must disapprove of teamwork. The question then might be heard with emphasis on the word, "enjoy," as criticism!

We could probably fill this book with possibilities based on a simple sentence. Many would unintentionally contribute to building a conflict. Let's go back to our model in Figure 1 to explore further how this can happen.

Words do not have meanings. Words are merely sounds. People assign meanings to them depending on their own definitions, experiences, and moods. Common words like "dependable," "judgment," "loyal," and "teamwork" have myriad meanings.

Even technical words can have multiple meanings. About ten years ago, I was called to assist two groups in a high-technology company who had been in conflict for over six years. They each believed their long-running disagreement had hurt their business because of the energy it consumed and because they could have taken on new types of projects if they had

A Sign of Health

Conflict itself is, of course, a sign of relative health as you would know if you ever met really apathetic people, really hopeless people, people who have given up hoping, striving, and coping.

Abraham Maslow[30]

learned to collaborate. This six-year-old conflict turned out to be entirely caused by *one* technical word that each group defined differently! (In fact, they were not even competing; they only thought they were because of the different definitions each held of this single word!)

Most attempts to measure how interpersonal messages are conveyed conclude that approximately 95 percent of the communication is nonverbal. Voice tone is usually a major component: I can call you a bum in a way that says "I love you" or "I hate you" depending mainly on my tone of voice (or entirely, if we are talking on the telephone).

Nonverbal cues—voice tone, body language, facial expression—are no more universal than verbal cues and are subject to as much misinterpretation. For example, by deliberately seeking feedback over the years, I have learned that I somehow give many people the impression that I am angry when, in fact, I am not. My facial expression, particularly when I am thinking hard, problem solving, or concentrating to understand a complicated presentation or idea, looks angry to some people. Merely by presenting me with a complex issue, they have come away believing they angered me! Unfortunately, I also convey what some interpret as anger when I'm depressed or not feeling well.

A psychotherapist might say that beneath depression hides anger and that some can sense it. That could be. In any case, I send a mixed message, one message with my words, another nonverbally. Mixed messages usually stem from a lack of congruence within one's self. They are familiar occurrences. When presented with such a message, people are most likely to believe the nonverbal message. Thus, the stereotypical used car salesperson says "good to meet you" with words and "you're nothing but a commission check to me, and I'm going to get you to buy this heap" nonverbally. Most of us are immediately on guard. Such mixed messages are likely to create credibility gaps and thereby feed future conflicts.

Negotiators have attempted to standardize nonverbal cues; for example, the bridging of one's hands (hands held in an expression of prayer but with palms separated) presumably indicates confidence. Such categorization is unreliable and, more importantly, unnecessary for those of us who don't make our living in formal negotiations. For us, nonverbal communications can most accurately be interpreted with the assistance of the person sending the message; how this is done will be described in the section called "Decoding Skills."

Other Factors

Another set of nonverbals sadly subject to interpretation (and misinterpretation) involves a person's physical presentation. Age, race, sex, mode of dress, hair style, odor, jewelry, weight, height, skirt length, tie width, *ad infinitum,* all communicate. It is hard to predict what they communicate because of the many stereotypes held in people's minds. Most of us try. We learn to "dress for success" and to conform to the cultural standards of our surroundings. These stereotypes are curiously potent barriers to communication, considering they actually have no functional impact in most cases. For example, think of the impact just a hat can have on most of us. Think of the possible repercussions from calling on most bank presidents impeccably dressed in a conservative business suit—and a baseball cap on your head. Or the incredible reactions to a slight patch of hair; a newly grown mustache or beard can enhance, or kill, a relationship! What a cap or bit of facial hair has to do with anything can be hard to fathom; nevertheless, we know the effect such apparently trivial matters can have on communications and conflict. People emotionally attribute meanings to such factors that override all attempts at logic.

I've worked with many people, perhaps the majority, whose ability even to notice, much less to interpret accurately, nonverbal communications is slight. Most don't realize this. They assume their interpretations are accurate, act on them, and often get into difficulties as a result.

The environment is generally assumed to be the same for each person if they are in the same location. However, for example, if the room or the weather is very warm, some people are energized and others impaired; some feel blessed and others are irritated and uncomfortable. Even the decor of a room can make a difference. Early American trappings convey and promote a mood of warmth and confident homeyness to some. To others it can trigger ugly and frightening feelings associated with a deprived childhood in a home with old furniture. Some people particularly enjoy, are stimulated by, and perform best in large groups; others are stifled in such settings and perform best in intimate, one-on-one encounters. Still others prefer to be with a small group of familiar friends, coworkers, or family members. The individual variations in response to surroundings are endless. Thus the environment can materially affect the quality of communications.

Magic

Those of us who have for years facilitated the in-depth workings of groups of people come to realize that much of what happens between people is beyond explanation. There is more to communication than all of the psychological, sociological, group dynamics, and interpersonal communications theories put together can explain. Call it vibes, E.S.P., chemistry, spirit, higher consciousness, or what you will, it is beyond our ordinary knowledge. Some of my colleagues and I, who are the leaders of a respected and long-running group dynamics educational experience offered by a major university, call it *magic*.

So, back to our seemingly simple sentence, "Do you enjoy teamwork?" The meaning conveyed depends upon verbal interpretations, nonverbal interpretations, reactions to surroundings, roles, qualities of the relationship, unconscious stereotyping, life histories, emotional states...and magic.

Decoding Skills

The sender, you or I in our everyday dealings, is actually sending a message in a secret code made up of all these factors. The receiver is faced with decoding the message, usually without benefit of a code book. We must be reminded of, or begin to grasp, the enormous challenge of our seemingly routine and ordinary communications. Thus the necessity of accepting the hard work of communicating is coupled with the necessity of accepting the inevitable losses of stability in a relationship. The two together help to explain why people who maintain vital, long-term marriages have had to learn that it takes lots of skillful, hard work. "Happily ever after" is only for fairy tales and old Hollywood movies. There's even more to this—the intrapersonal issues—that we'll consider later.

> *The ability to care is also associated*
> *with one's willingness to see—or want to*
> *see, for that matter—another person's*
> *point of view or needs and act*
> *accordingly.*
>
> Jack Beasley

Just as paraphrasing is a simple (conceptually, at least) method of decoding the meanings of words, there are simple means for decoding nonverbal signals. The sender's feelings generate nonverbal signals. Therefore, senders can encode their nonverbal signals by including a *description of feelings* in their messages. In other words, if the message has an emotional content, the sender will do well to clarify it. For example, "you left the door unlocked" can carry lots of meanings depending upon whether you appreciate the unlocked door, are upset by confronting the locked door, frightened without the security of knowing the door is locked, or extremely angry because this is the tenth time you've had to say it. To encode the message, simply say, "You left the door unlocked and I am glad/upset/ frightened/mad as hell."

In my case, when I'm concentrating, I've learned to say, "I'm not angry, I just look that way when I'm concentrating." I've watched a number of people breathe a sigh of relief after hearing me say so.

Similarly, rather than assume you know or can read the sender's nonverbal message, you can simply *check your perception* by asking for a decoding. "You look angry; are you?" "You seemed displeased by what I just said; are you?" "I sense you are committed to the project; am I right?" "You seem concerned and I'm wondering why?" "You seem pleased with my offer, is that true?"

If people would describe feelings and check perceptions more often, we'd have more efficient and effective communications, and fewer conflicts, in the world.

We will now proceed with more how-to's of effective conflict management.

Moral: The seemingly familiar and
ordinary act of everyday
communication is actually an
extraordinarily complex and
obscure process. Consider
miscommunication as routine
and part of the process. Expect
communication to be challenging
and patiently work at it.

II
P   A   R   T

CONFRONTING OTHERS

Two Sets of Problems

Let us think of the individual as a unified system with two sets of problems—one the problem of maintaining inner harmony within himself, and the other the problem of maintaining harmony with the environment, especially the social environment, in the midst of which he lives.

Clark Moustakas[43]

$\mathbf{P}$art II is for the many busy and practical-minded people who want to take the shortest possible route to improvement in their personal and professional relations. I will proceed as directly as I can to tell the reader how to prevent most differences with others from becoming destructive conflicts whereby a friend, a spouse, a customer, a key employee, a promotion, a job, or other valued relationship is lost. Part III will add to and extend this material for those who may enjoy more in-depth understanding.

Image to Image

In all our relationships each one of us builds an image about the other and these two images have a relationship, not the human beings themselves. The wife has an image about the husband—perhaps not consciously but never-the-less it is there—and the husband has an image about the wife. One has an image about one's country and about oneself, and we are always strengthening these images by adding more and more to them. And it is these images which have the relationship. The actual relationship between two human beings or between many human beings completely ends when there is the formation of images.

J. Krishnamurti[28]

4
C   H   A   P   T   E   R

ESTABLISHING STABILITY

The first thing to learn in intercourse with others is non-interference with their own peculiar ways of being happy, provided those ways do not assume to interfere by violence with ours.

William James

Before we get to the how-to's, we have to remind ourselves of what goes into the establishment of a relationship. Generally, we put relatively large amounts of energy into initiating and building a relationship. The amount of energy depends upon the importance of the relationship. For instance, when we are interviewing for a job, we make sure we are well groomed and appropriately dressed. We do our homework so we know enough to ask good questions and are clear about what we're looking for. We go through the interview process on our best behavior, doing our utmost to create a favorable impression with everyone we meet. We follow up the interview process with carefully crafted notes and tactful telephone calls. After being hired, we come to work on our toes and are keenly alert to every signal pointing the way to early success. We dress the part, talk the part, play the part, and eventually, become the part. All this takes lots of energy. Likewise, when we're courting romantically, we work to make everything perfect: the place, the setting, the time, the wine, our looks, even the way we smell and the cars we drive.

Another view of the same phenomena is the energy demanded when a valued relationship goes awry. Experienced managers know that one problem employee can take up more time and energy than all of the others together. Similarly, we all have experienced a primary relationship in trouble; again, the anguish and involvement can dominate one's life until the problems are resolved.

On the other hand, relatively unimportant relationships take little energy to establish and maintain. A carpool, for example, may require only an agreement to be punctual.

Avoiding True Communication

*An avoidance of true communication is tantamount
to a relinquishment of my self-being; if I withdraw
from it I am betraying not only the other but
myself.*

Karl Jaspers[20]

What we seek, after all, in any relationship is stability. Stability is established when each person involved has sufficient confidence in the respective levels of commitment of the others to the relationship. Once the new hire has stood out as an effective contributor—and knows it—and the manager has the confidence of the employee—and knows it—a reasonable degree of stability is established between them. Once the courtship is over and a mutual success, and the couple has established a mutually satisfactory mode of cohabitation, they each feel confident of a stable union.

Stability has at least two key characteristics: it is comfortable for the parties involved, and the energy required to establish or repair, as the case may be, is now available for other use. The manager and the employee have clear-enough mutual expectations governing behavior and sufficient confidence in each other to stop giving primary attention to their relationship; each can now apply that time and attention to other projects. Likewise, the new couple enjoys enough certainty in their relationship for each to go their own way and pursue their respective interests without worrying about what the other may be thinking or doing.

In summary, stability is achieved when the respective roles and commitments are clear enough to the members of the relationship. "Clear enough" because the evidence of clarity and commitment required also depends upon the nature of the members. People who operate at high levels of trust may require relatively little—a handshake, a verbal agreement, a nod, a kiss. Others may require written agreements to be comfortable. Most want some combination of tangible and intangible symbols, formal and informal agreements, before feeling fully confident—again, depending on the perceived importance of the relationship.

"Everything is fine and we're each getting what we want from the relationship." That's stability. And that's a good, warm feeling. And it *never* lasts. There's the rub.

It does not last because seldom, if ever, is full, mutual understanding achieved at the start in important relationships and/or because circumstances change and/or because people change. Let's briefly consider these possibilities in this order.

People rarely work hard to establish clear expectations in the early stages of a relationship, no matter how important. Most of us are not schooled to do so, and even if we were, it often seems more friendly and more comfortable not to push for too much specificity. Hence, although the manager and new employee may get very specific about such impersonal issues as working hours and wage scales, potential trouble areas like management styles, accountability, communication requirements, and personal preferences get glossed over. In fact, it is common to hear new employees speak of "psyching out" the boss, meaning reading verbal and nonverbal cues to the boss's likes and dislikes. This is a very iffy, inevitably inaccurate way of setting expectations that make mutual sense. Similarly, the romantic beginnings of most marriages and modern live-together arrangements tend to preclude clarity about the mechanics of cohabitation and mutual anticipations of the couple.

Thus the possibility for apparent breaches of all kinds is created early in the relationship. For example, the new employee gives the manager the impression of being interested in a managerial career with the organization when, in fact, the employee's fondest hope for the future is a business of his or her own. The employee may do a great job while building a nest egg toward a new business. If the manager wants to promote the employee while the employee is getting ready to depart, a major misunderstanding is likely to erupt. A more typical example is the manager who courts an employee overenthusiastically with promises of opportunities so unlikely that they never materialize. Also typical are couples who contemplate cohabitation or marriage, but don't consider up-front clarity about wants, hence their stability is usually shaky and based on romantic illusions.

Regardless of how carefully a relationship is set up, sooner or later shifting circumstances undermine even the sweetest of beginnings. In a work situation, a budget cut, for example, can produce ramifications detrimental to stability. A change of ownership, management, markets, the economy—an almost infinite array of factors—can alter the nature and requirements of even well-established relationships, particularly between managers and employees. Similarly, the birth of the first child usually strongly affects the relationship between husband and wife because the helpless baby necessarily becomes the center of attention and first priority. (Even household pets may react to their change of status when a new baby arrives!)

And people change. As a result of the inevitable crises in life, of learning, of aging, their expectations and values shift. Thus, what was once okay or even highly valued in a relationship is no longer wanted. For example, in the early days of the modern women's movement, some women in secretarial positions found their jobs frustrating after attending a consciousness raising workshop. "Why should I make the coffee and wash the cups? My boss can take a turn at making coffee and wash his own cup!" They had experienced a change of values—hence, expectations—that often caught their bosses off guard, sometimes messing up a previously acceptable relationship. I've heard many people who have suffered through, sought help for, and grown as a consequence of a divorce say they would never be the same person they once were. As a result, they look for different sorts of relationships. Particularly during the 1970s (and even today) people sought out personal growth experiences, some of which led to changing expectations about relationships.

Stability will *inevitably* be shaken by new discoveries, by changes in circumstances, and by changes in expectations. This shift in stability is often first experienced as some sort of restriction of freedom, a breach of a promise, or "pinch": a remark or look taken as a put down, a project delivered late or over budget, an indication that a contribution to the job or home is of a lower value than expected, a complaint about some activity or relationship. Sometimes the slightest nod at the wrong time, or the toothpaste tube squeezed in the "wrong" way, or the cap left off a bottle will push a button that starts a downward spiral to a destructive conflict. It's not so much the triggering event or pinch, but the response that leads to trouble.

Moral: Important, long-term relationships are subject to an endless series of changes and problems. Real people don't live "happily ever after." Relationships require maintenance.

The Wall

Increasingly, I have become painfully aware of the ter-
ribleness of most communication; of people talking
but not saying what they mean; of the contradiction
between the outward words and expressions and the
inner meanings and messages; of people looking as
if they were listening without any real connection or
contact with one another.

Clark Moustakas[42]

BUILDING THE WALL

Were half the power that fills the world with
terror,
Were half the wealth bestowed on camp and
courts,
Given to redeem the human mind from error,
There would be no need of arsenals nor forts.
Henry Wadsworth Longfellow

Let's say the pinch is a dirty look or perceived snub of some sort. Although nothing more may be known but that, the human mind abhors a vacuum and will rush to fill itself with assumptions, motives, and conclusions. Once such a conclusion has been generated, the need to be right—not to be wrong and therefore in a position to be criticized, or even not to be crazy (these are the alternatives to being right)—takes over and a destructive conflict is in the making. The mind creates—and creates and creates and creates—thus veiling reality. Trying to stop it is like trying to ride a bucking bull; if you're good you might do so for a few seconds before it throws you and goes on its way. Most of the mind's creations are negative (although we all experience positive fantasies, which nonetheless obscure what is). In fact, the mind is addicted to negativity. This has been recognized for thousands of years. If you will pay attention to your thoughts, chances are you will notice that it's so.

For example, years ago I worked in a laboratory as a researcher in microwave electronics and solid state physics. My boss was a man named Al. One day, as I was walking through our parking lot toward the lab, I met Al coming the other way. I greeted him and smiled. He looked toward me with an apparently angry look on his face and said nothing; he just walked on by. His look pushed a button: although all I knew was that he had walked by without responding to me and that he appeared angry, my mind didn't settle for that. Immediately, my mind, with the help of my ego, analyzed: my ego compared my work performance against its own

The Origin of Conflict

The origin of all conflict between me and my fellow men is that I do not say what I mean, and that I do not do what I say.

Martin Buber[5]

impossible standards and my mind went to work. "Oh, oh," I thought, "there's something wrong. Al has a problem with me. It probably has something to do with my not being a great analyst." There's the germ or seed of potential future conflict: once we form a perception, we must prove it to be correct. Because life is so complex, we can invariably find enough data to support our foregone conclusions. That's why everyone is virtually always "right." I was no exception.

The next day as I was walking in, I again met Al. I greeted him and his response virtually repeated the previous day. Right away my ego-mind latched onto that and generated a whole list of negative possibilities about my performance and stature in his eyes. Three days later I passed Al in the hallway inside the lab. The same thing happened. By then, my mental scenario had me about to be fired because "although I was a good experimentalist, I didn't approach my work from a sufficiently analytical basis; my work wasn't central to the future of the lab; and Al, who was Canadian by birth, liked Cecil, one of my Canadian colleagues, better than me."

Let me digress here to point out that the epitome of making myself right would have been to get myself fired. We create our own world maps by making our ideas about what's true come true. I could have done so, perhaps unconsciously, by acting resentful and distant around my boss, by demoralizing myself, by losing confidence, and/or by otherwise reducing my effectiveness and productivity.

Fortunately, I finally went in and asked Al what was going on. (These days, if I catch my mind building a scenario, I don't wait.) Al was surprised; he hadn't even noticed me in the parking lot or in the hall. He had been deeply immersed in his own thoughts. He told me that he had recently been diagnosed with a serious illness and that his wife was filing for a divorce. No wonder he was preoccupied and had such a look on his face; he was hurting. My ego-mind, in its wild, negative imaginings narcissistically focused on what was "wrong" with me. I didn't look with any compassion or empathy at Al and the possibility that he was in trouble.

Major conflicts typically occur as the result of a minor incident that acts as a seed: a facial expression, remark, or word used in a memo is interpreted in a negative way. The need to be right sets the interpreter on an unconscious quest for data confirming the initial interpretation. Because of the richness of life and the selective perception employed, the confirmation is assured (often actually created by some act or acts in conformance with the perception), and the seed grows into a full-fledged conflict.

A stone wall is a particularly appropriate metaphor. Like a stone wall, conflicts are built stone by stone. The stones in interpersonal conflicts are actions *perceived* as insulting, breaches of trust, ignoring, irritating, misunderstanding, discounting, mistakes, and so forth. Sooner or later, the Wall stands and is very hard to breach. For example, I helped trace a serious conflict between a top-level manager and the four middle managers reporting to him to an expression on the top manager's face. This occurred some years ago when I conducted a team building session for these five managers, who were starting a new department. We had a very successful three-day session launching their business and building a managerial team. We agreed to a follow-on meeting three months later.

I next encountered the four junior managers just prior to the follow-on. All were extremely angry with their boss, the department manager. They agreed he had betrayed them. He had promised them a trip to a conference in Europe, and they had planned to take their families along. They said that in spite of his professed desire for participative decisions, he had arbitrarily and unilaterally cancelled the trips. The Wall was solidly in place.

I spoke with the boss. He was dumfounded by this news. In his view nothing had changed. He had not cancelled the trips.

When the entire group got together, it took some time for these people to come to grips with this apparently bizarre situation. I suggested that, since all of the actors in the drama were together and the misunderstanding had occurred entirely during the previous three months, we attempt to trace its origin. (My objective was to establish firm credibility between the boss and the others, as well as to have us learn whatever we could from the experience.) It took four and a half hours of arduous effort to trace the beginning of the misconception to a conversation one of the junior managers had with the boss. Near the end of the conversation the trip had been mentioned and, according to the junior manager, "The boss gave me a dirty look."

This dirty look was the seed that grew into a full-fledged fantasy shared by four very intelligent people, the stone that started the Wall. The junior manager interpreted the "dirty look" in the light of a rumor he'd heard about budget problems and unconsciously set out to make his half-conscious assumptions right. Anyone can find commiserators to bolster his or her views, and he had three who were ready. By the time we had our

Gunnysacking the Pinches

*Sulky people are hard to appease, and retain their
anger long; for they repress their passion. But it
ceases when they retaliate; for revenge relieves them
of their anger, producing in them pleasure instead of
pain. If this does not happen they retain their
burden; for owing to its not being obvious no one
ever reasons with them, and to digest one's anger in
oneself takes time.*

Aristotle[39]

follow-on meeting they were all in agreement, had a clear and detailed picture of the situation, and were as mad as could be. Independently, I could not have found a loop-hole in their story: as always, every "i" was dotted and every "t" crossed with impeccable logic—they were "right." The only trouble was, of course, that they had constructed a reality that bore no relation to the actual facts. The boss's dirty look had been caused by the thought of an argument he'd had earlier that day outside the office.

Mind reading the motives of others is the source of countless unnecessary and destructive conflicts. In this situation, the dirty look was *interpreted* as relating to the European trips. Subsequent discussions and observations by the four managers were *perceived* by them to verify this interpretation, building the Wall between them and their boss. They believed their agreement to be a rational confirmation of accuracy. (As previously mentioned, once such an interpretation is made, the unconscious need to be right takes over and data is gathered accordingly.) Characteristically, none of the four managers even considered checking out his perception with the boss; the boss said nothing about the trip because, in his view, nothing had changed.

Rarely can a conflict be traced to its first stone. In this case, we were able to do so because everyone involved was together and anxious to attempt it, and because relatively little time had passed. Even so, tracing the process backwards, step by step, was painstaking. I believe we were lucky to accomplish it. None of us will ever forget it.

The requirements for effective conflict management are (1) the recognition that breaches of stability in relationships are inevitable and (2) the full acceptance of personal responsibility for one's own actions and reactions to these pinches. Each is an essential requirement for the successful management of relationships, particularly long-term and important ones.

Stability cannot last. When handled effectively, pinches can strengthen the relationship. See them as opportunities because they signal that an adjustment is needed, that maintenance is required to prevent a future breakdown.

Moral: Significant destructive conflicts
are almost invariably the result
of many seemingly minor issues
not dealt with as they occur. We
must be willing to confront the
small stuff if big conflicts are
to be prevented. Don't let Walls
be built.

Don't Be A Victim

One can spend a lifetime assigning blame, finding the causes "out there" for all troubles that exist. Contrast this with the "responsible attitude" of confronting the situation, bad or good, and, instead of asking "What caused the trouble? Who was to blame?" asking "How can I handle this present situation best to make the most of it? What can I salvage here?"

Abraham Maslow[34]

6

C H A P T E R

THE VICTIM ATTITUDE

Unto whomsoever much is given,
of him shall much be required.
Luke 12:48

When some apparent breach—a stone that might begin a Wall—occurs, the person who experiences it must take some action. This requires taking full, personal responsibility at the moment. It requires us to acknowledge our reactions—our thoughts, assumptions, and feelings. We cannot adopt a "victim" attitude: blame the other person and wait for some rescuer. This point is well worth emphasizing because it is probably the greatest source of self-limiting behavior and almost guaranteed to develop destructive conflicts sooner or later.

The role of a victim, in this sense, is determined by one's own attitude, not by any outside oppressor or persecutor. It derives entirely from avoiding personal responsibility. Let's say a project manager is dependent, for the success of her project, on the procurement department obtaining a certain part by a certain date. The date arrives and the part does not. A victim response by the project manager would be something like, "The procurement department did not get the part, so it's their fault that I can't get my project done on time."

The project manager who does not accept the victim's role would respond to the same situation by retaining full, personal responsibility: "The part did not come in; now, what do I do?" The project manager fully owns her responsibility to get the job done and begins a search for other ways of doing so.

The nonvictim response is not a Pollyanna avoidance maneuver. The project manager does not overlook the possibility that the Procurement department did, indeed, fail to do its job. She simply includes that possibility in her problem-solving response to the crisis.

Another common example of victim behavior is the person who complains that his boss or spouse "walks all over me." The victim or "aggressee" refuses to recognize that such behavior (physical violence is not considered here) is possible only with his cooperation—he must "lie down" so the "aggressor" can "walk on" him. They must dance together or the dance would end.

> *It is a painful thing to look at your own*
> *trouble and know that you yourself and*
> *no one else has made it.*
> Sophocles (c. 447 B.C.)

The debilitating aspect of the victim attitude stems primarily from the personal power the victim thereby gives away. The attitude invariably involves blaming and waiting for some rescuer to relieve the situation. Thus, victims create their own helplessness. In the previous example of the project manager, the persecutor is Procurement and the logical rescuer would be management. (Again, Procurement may indeed need managerial attention. The victim will merely blame; the responsible project manager will initiate some corrective action, perhaps on the part of management.) Considering the aggressor-aggressee example, the hoped-for rescuer could again be management, family members or others, depending upon the specific situation.

Skillful victims—I call them "professional victims" (the psychological term is "character disorder")—in most cases can't be relieved of many of their problems by the usual means. Managers, friends, relatives, even psychotherapists, must eventually fail to be of assistance because the victims succeed in blaming others and won't assume responsibility. In one sadly memorable conflict management session that I facilitated between such a person, a senior scientist, and his boss, we got nowhere because the scientist was such a skillful victim. We would zero in on a point of contention between the scientist and the manager only to have the scientist adroitly shift blame to the organization. Once we clarified and focused in on the organizational issue as he defined it, he switched to blaming the scientific profession. Concentrating here produced a shift to blaming Western civilization. And so it went, until the manager and I simply had to give up.

We all behave as victims now and then because of the rewards we reap for successfully doing so. In the long run such rewards fall in the category a colleague of mine would call "crummy." A list of the victim's crummy rewards appears in Figure 2.

One common crummy reward is commiseration. The project manager could turn to a colleague and tell her sad tale. This may give the colleague a chance to join in complaining about Procurement or even topping her story. For victims, commiseration feels good. It's a chummy

interaction that produces a sort of closeness. Mostly, the reward is to rein-
force being right and to protect the victim from the possible discovery
of having made a mistake. The commiserators make each other right and
join in feeling righteous by gossiping about (rather than confronting) the
Procurement department. If the project manager did confront Procurement,
chances are she would find that she contributed in some way to the late
delivery, perhaps by ordering too late or trying to circumvent the procurement cycle in some way.

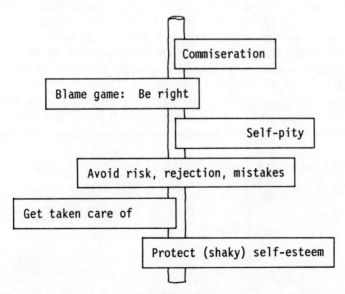

Figure 2.   The Victim's (Crummy) Rewards

Victims, by themselves and/or with commiserators, invariably play the blame game so they can be right. This is basic victim behavior that allows them to avoid responsibility and protect themselves from being criticized. By avoiding contact with the many possible aspects of the issue, some of which may expose some imperfection on their part, they successfully, blindly, and comfortably, remain "right."

Self-pity is another crummy reward for some victims. "Poor me" adds the justification for self-nurturance in the face of persecution and is highly disempowering. Once again, however, the person can bathe in righteousness, avoid dealing with the issues, and stay "right."

The next two crummy rewards listed move progressively closer to the real reward of victim behavior, protecting self-esteem. Victim behavior is protection from the possibility of experiencing rejection or (knowing about) making a mistake. Its many forms are manipulations that, when successful, allow the victim to remain the irresponsible child who is rescued or taken care of by some parent figure—and which of us doesn't want to be taken care of now and then?

Victim behavior, although highly debilitating to personal effectiveness in every arena of life, is prevalent because it essentially stems from the sense of inadequacy we all carry. We all suffer, to some degree, from shaky self-esteem. Playing the victim protects us from confronting and dealing with our own negative feelings. (This means, of course, that the big crummy reward is the avoidance of personal growth!)

An exercise used for the past 40 years or so in growth groups tells the story. At a time when the participants are experiencing a very high level of mutual trust, the trainer hands out 3x5 cards. The trainer's instructions are for the participants to write on one side of the card something they least would like others to know about them, and on the other that which they most wished others to know. The overwhelming majority of "negative" entries express some sense of inadequacy or incompetence. The positive entries are typically a version of "If you only knew me, you'd love me."

> *The Fault, dear Brutus, is not in our
> stars, but in ourselves, that we are
> underlings.*
> *Shakespeare* (Julius Caesar)

Moral: Recognize that we can only be victims by choice. Choose to be fully responsible for all of your reactions and actions. We must stop blaming and settling for the victim's crummy rewards.

On Accepting Criticism

The person who is criticized honestly may be hurt for the moment, but ultimately he is helped and cannot but become grateful. Anyway, it's a great sign of respect to me, for instance, if someone feels I'm strong enough, capable enough, and objective enough so that he can tell me where I've pulled a boner. It's only those people who regard me as delicate, sensitive, or weak, or fragile who will not dare to disagree with me.

Abraham Maslow[28]

7
C H A P T E R

FACING DIFFERENCES

You must turn and face the tiger to learn it is made of paper.

Zen saying

Differences are an expected part of life with other people. They are neither bad nor good, but simply natural. Growing up to the full acceptance of personal responsibility for all aspects of one's own personal set of circumstances, including conflicts, is the *sine qua non* of vital and dynamic relationships.

Once we are willing to accept the inevitable problems that are part of every long-lived relationship of any consequence and to assume full responsibility for our lives, we face the next barrier in effectively managing conflict. We face the paradox that the primary sources of most major or destructive conflicts are (1) the avoidance of confronting, or expressing and working through, differences and (2) the need to be right.

Avoidance is to be expected. After all, stability is characterized by comfort, by a sense of assurance, security, and commitment. A breach of stability is typically accompanied by discomfort, by anxiety, ambiguity, uncertainty, and anger. It is natural enough, therefore, to want to return to a state of comfort by the most direct route possible. The usual first reaction is to attempt to ignore the breach, saying it was nothing, apologizing without dealing with the underlying hurt, or perhaps hugging or shaking hands without real heart-felt contact.

Our avoidance takes many forms. Some are listed in Figure 3. The list is certainly not exhaustive and some of the items are interrelated.

Perhaps the most basic source of avoidance is fear, fear of discomfort and fear of harming the relationship. Both are understandable and justified. For most of us, expressing a difference is uncomfortable and unpleasant, perhaps frightening. To avoid the unpleasantness of fear, one common strategy is to build up anger. This, of course, almost always results in an ineffectual expression of the issue and an exacerbation of the problem.

The avoidance, itself, precludes the necessity for skill development. The lack of conflict management skills and the avoidance of confrontation are a chicken-egg situation. Furthermore, even the most skillful expression of a difference to some particularly defensive people can, in fact, ruin a workable relationship—there are no panaceas here.

A favorite form of avoidance is to tell one's self there is not enough time to deal with the difference. Sometimes that is the truth, but more often merely an excuse. Another favorite is to tell one's self that this little irritation or issue isn't important enough to fret about (while ignoring the knot in the stomach, the headache coming on, or the thoughts of revenge). A variation is to say to yourself that the issue isn't important enough to bother the other person about, particularly if the other person is someone who has authority over you.

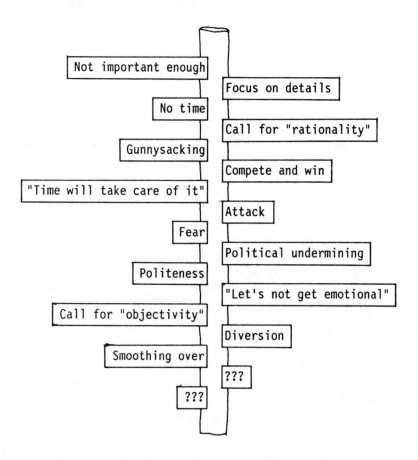

Figure 3. Some Forms of Avoidance

On Asserting Oneself

For if one is unable to assert oneself, one is unable to participate in a genuine relationship.

Rollo May[35]

We all know about political maneuvering or undermining as a means of avoiding face-to-face encounters, although many people fail to realize the avoidance angle. Even the familiar Roberts Rules of Order are a means of avoiding the necessity of skillful confrontation. Politeness, too, is used as a means of avoidance. We all know how to pretend tactfully that everything is okay. Most of us are well schooled in knowing how to smile and shake hands even with people we can't stand.

Another means of avoidance—particularly among engineers, scientists, lawyers, accountants, and men in general—is to call for "objectivity" or "rationality." "Let's not get emotional" is a favorite statement. Most of these people fail to realize that "rational" in the sense they use the term means "agreeing with my views." They also typically ignore the fact that suppressing the expression of feelings usually precludes objectivity because the feelings will operate anyway to influence viewpoints and decisions, but outside of one's awareness. Feelings must be acknowledged for rationality or objectivity to be truly manifested.

Another favorite avoidance by this group, and so called "left-brained" people in general, is to focus on details. I've seen many a team building session get off to a slow start because the participants focused on word definitions and technical fine points.*

Some people avoid by "oiling the water," by diverting or smoothing over the issue. "Everything will be fine, don't worry about it." "Let's talk about something else." "Oh, it's just human nature." "Go to the movies, you'll feel better." "Let's not rock the boat."

"Gunnysacking" is a highly descriptive term we owe to Virginia Satir, the noted family therapist.** It means storing grievances as if in

---

*The observations expressed in this and the preceding paragraph are substantially simplified. A more comprehensive treatment can be found in *Please Understand Me*, David Kiersey and Marilyn Bates (Prometheus Nemesis Books, 1984), and in *Gifts Differing*, Isabel Briggs Myers (Consulting Psychologists Press, 1980).

**Virginia Satir was a pioneer family therapist whose work and writings strongly contributed to the understanding of group dynamics. Her books include: *Peoplemaking* (1972), *Self Esteem: A Declaration* (1975), *Changing with Families* (1976), *Helping Families to Change* (1976), *Making Contact* (1976), *Your Many Faces* (1978), *Cojoint Family Therapy* (1982), *Satir Step by Step* (1984), *Meditation and Inspirations* (1985).

Two Dimensions of Behavior

Unless the capacity for compassion-through-understanding: is supplemented by the capacity for anger, disapproval, and indignation, the result may be a flattening of all affect, a blandness in reaction to people, an inability to be indignant, and a loss of discrimination of and taste for real capacity, skill, superiority, and excellence.

Abraham Maslow[33]

---

a gunnysack and carrying the sack around slung over the shoulder. One day, just a look or remark fills the sack, and we dump the whole thing in front of the other person. I can still remember one such episode when I made a remark that irritated my wife. This was "the straw that broke the camel's back" and she proceeded to dump her gunnysack: "...and the way you behaved in front of the furniture store in San Jose in 1963..!" I couldn't even remember being near any furniture store, much less my behavior. We're all familiar with gunnysacking and the nearly impossible task of sorting out what to do with the contents once they are dumped.

Instead of confronting effectively, we can avoid by competing, taking a win-lose approach, even by being aggressive and attacking. The former is common in our culture, and the latter is often viewed as the only alternative to avoidance. Neither of these is truly a useful long-term strategy; fortunately, as we shall see, neither is necessary.

We can avoid by gossiping and commiserating as discussed previously under the victim's crummy rewards.

All but a handful of the thousands of conflicts I have dealt with was built as a stone wall is built, stone by stone. Each stone is typically small, and as is the case of a real stone wall, the Wall built by them can be large, strong, and seemingly impossible to climb or circumvent. The process whereby the Wall is built is essentially the gunnysacking process. It is depicted in Figure 4.

The actual Wall building process is usually hidden from view. Most of us build such Walls without being aware of doing so. Hence, the process is known more by its consequences, by the existence of the Wall and by the experience of taking it down, than by viewing its erection.

The first stone is often not of major consequence in itself. My favorite example is the toothpaste tube in my house while my three sons were growing up. My wife and the boys squeezed the tube almost anywhere, usually in the middle. They often left the cap off so a certain amount of toothpaste dribbled onto the counter. I am not particularly neat by nature, but my way was to squeeze the tube from the bottom and roll it up carefully as the contents expired. Given my strong philosophical bent, it would seem I would overlook such a trivial issue. However, I'm a bit embarrassed to admit I didn't; I fussed and fumed for several years about that messy tube. It bugged me! Fortunately, before we had built a significant "toothpaste-tube Wall" between us, squeeze by squeeze, we built a separate bathroom for me! I got my very own toothpaste tube to squeeze my way and never had to even look at their squishy version again. (If only all such differences were resolvable by such simple, mechanical adjustments!)

Almost any incident, interpreted negatively, can serve as the beginning of a Wall. If the incident is not faced and dealt with effectively, doubt is established and the trust required for stability is shaken a bit. This doubt or breach of trust, however slight, can trigger an unconscious search

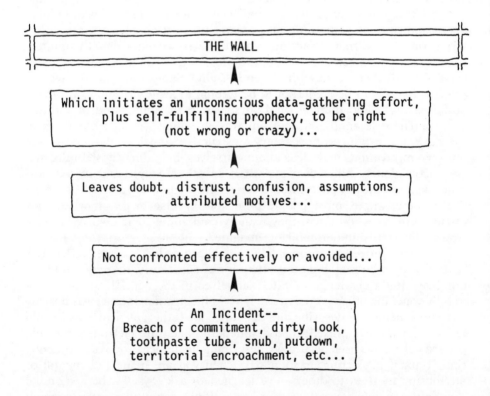

THE WALL

Which initiates an unconscious data-gathering effort,
plus self-fulfilling prophecy, to be right
(not wrong or crazy)...

Leaves doubt, distrust, confusion, assumptions,
attributed motives...

Not confronted effectively or avoided...

An Incident--
Breach of commitment, dirty look,
toothpaste tube, snub, putdown,
territorial encroachment, etc...

Figure 4. Building the Wall: How Conflict is Established

for verification. Because of the infinite richness of human life and the unlimited capacity of the mind to create what it believes is true, most such searches are unfortunately successful.

Via a well-known process called the "self-fulfilling prophecy," the person often will cause the perceived reaction to, in fact, occur. Suppose, for example, that Jack concludes from a fleeting expression on her face that Ann doesn't like him. How does he respond? Chances are he'll become—perhaps ever so slightly at first—on his guard around Ann. He's not as open and warm around her as he could be. She, of course, senses his reserve and pulls away from him. That's how the self-fulfilling cycle begins. He reads her pulling back as confirmation of his original expectation and becomes even more reserved. She (while perhaps wondering what's wrong) withdraws further. And so it goes. Chances are, pretty soon she won't like him, even though the original look on her face that started it all may actually have had nothing to do with him. And he will have made himself right; hence, this process is aptly named the "self-fulfilling prophecy." He created and caused to happen what he thought was happening.

I want to belabor the fact that once we formulate an idea or opinion about someone or something, if we don't prove it correct, we are either wrong or crazy. Either is very uncomfortable, so we will—usually unintentionally and unconsciously—set out to prove it true. Chances are we'll succeed. We will thereby stay blind—and "right." Sadly, most people will go to great lengths to be right, not to be wrong, to avoid criticism. We make ourselves right and thereby keep ourselves in the dark—and in conflict.

There is another important way in which we keep ourselves in the dark and produce unnecessary, destructive conflicts. We tend to see our own motivations and ideas about ourselves, including those faults that we unconsciously hide from ourselves, in other people and in our surroundings. We project parts of our secret selves onto the "screens" of others. Since, for example, most people have nothing else to go on when they attribute motives to others, they usually contribute their own. What else would they truly understand or imagine?

This process, appropriately called "projection," creates reflections that appear to be real. We do it often, if not constantly, thereby muddling our lives. It's a challenge to catch ourselves in the act. I first caught on to it by watching others. A particularly vivid illustration, for me, was hearing a friend vehemently describe and denounce his father; as nearly as I could tell, my friend was presenting a detailed and accurate picture of himself. (He may also have been accurately describing his father.) You will frequently find yourself projecting, particularly when you are being judgmental or attributing motives to others. I've learned to ask myself whether or not I'm doing so whenever I say (or even think) something critical about someone else. Each time I find myself projecting, I free myself from the

The most effective and the most healthy way to produce change in the other person is to ask him to change.

Sidney Jourard[23]

act, because I can't continue to project blindly once I am aware of what I'm doing.

Your world is actually a kind of self-portrait. You can test this for yourself. One of the easiest ways to see the process of projection at work is to recall someone who bugs you, who rubs you the wrong way, whom you can't stand. On a sheet of paper, quickly list the characteristics of the person that you find repulsive. Then cross out his or her name and substitute your own. See what you find. I've often asked people in my workshops to try the same exercise with inanimate objects: think of the place where you live, and list the characteristics of your most and least favorite parts of your dwelling place. Then put your own name at the head of both lists and see what you discover. What you think and say about virtually anyone or anything, particularly that which you denounce most strongly, is likely to include a reflection of your view of yourself.

This is frequently true of people who are in conflict. When Max tells me about Beth, about what she is like and why, I've learned that I may or may not actually be hearing a description of her. I am most certainly hearing something about Max. Check yourself the next time you criticize, attribute motives to, or are irritated by the actions of another; see if you are in some way describing yourself.

> *Each of us understands in others only those feelings he is capable of producing himself.*
>
> *André Gide*

Figure 5 depicts the Wall. Walls, as in the first example in this book (page 8), can be built from an irritating mannerism that is repeated over and over again. Or they can be erected by a sequence of many different events. Once they are in place, they are very difficult to deal with because of their complexity and/or the behaviors that have contributed to their construction. Once a Wall is up, the builders usually need help to tear it down.

Thus, a key to effective conflict management, to keeping relationships vital and preventing destructive conflicts, is to *confront every issue now* (or as close to "now" as possible). *Do not avoid them.* We need the skills to do this effectively. In addition, managers need to set an example and coach subordinates to express their differences with others directly and work through them at the earliest possible stage.

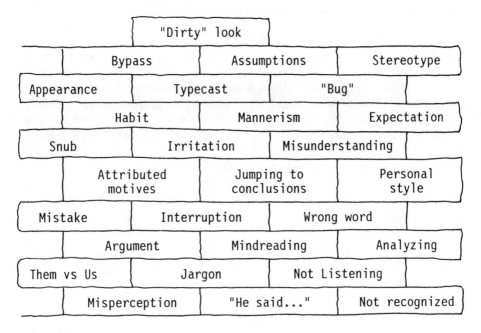

Figure 5. The Wall

Moral: It will pay to learn exactly how you avoid conflict and thereby contribute to the erection of Walls. Noting precisely how we talk ourselves out of facing differences and catching on to projection are important. Check yourself carefully for the almost universal need to be right.

Two Ways to Confront

There are, then, two ways to confront or criticize another human being: with instinctive and spontaneous certainty that one is right, or with a belief that one is probably right arrived at through scrupulous self-doubting and self-examination. The first is the way of arrogance.... The second is the way of humility....

M. Scott Peck[44]

CHAPTER 8

CONFLICT MANAGEMENT SKILLS

*How do we determine the golden mean or
excellent action? The faculty required is wisdom.
Aristotle, in his discourses, identified two types of
wisdom, theoretical and practical. We must
develop and utilize each to actualize our potential.*
                                        Beverly A. Potter

The first jarring note in a relationship that has enjoyed a period of stability usually is experienced by only one of the parties. Some people are sensitive: they easily pick up the smallest cue and quickly react at the feeling level. Some, it seems, have to be hit over the head before they notice anything. In any event, their partner in the relationship, their colleague or whomever, typically is not aware that anything has happened. If a future Wall is to be prevented, the offended person must deal with the pinch; he or she must say something about it.

The alternative is to let go of the issue or forgive the other person. Since the occasion of forgiveness arises because one person expects or wants something of the other, true forgiveness is rare. Thus, the "pinchee" usually must assume full responsibility for his or her feelings and be prepared to express them. In a previous example (page 24), the secretary who now resents making coffee is the only one aware of her resentment. Blaming others or assuming "they should know" would be to play the victim.

The need to express one's sense of being restricted, put down, rejected, insulted, overlooked, unappreciated, slighted, confused, hurt, betrayed, bored, manipulated, or any other pinch brings us to the first of the conflict management skills: learning to *describe behavior* rather than to attribute and describe motives. Consider, for example, an ordinary event—a morning business meeting of about a dozen people including

A Mutual Search for Truth

For I imagine we are not striving merely to secure victory for my suggestions or for yours; rather we ought both of us to fight in support of the truth and the whole truth.

Socrates[45]

Chuck and Dave. They are seated around a table in a conference room. The boss presents a problem and the discussion begins.

Shortly after the outset of the group discussion, Chuck opens his mouth to speak. Scarcely has he uttered a sound when Dave speaks up loudly and forcefully, apparently ignoring Chuck. Chuck feels cut off by Dave and shuts up. Chuck immediately tries to make sense of Dave's behavior: perhaps Dave wants to impress the boss, or Dave is mad because he found out that Chuck went to see Dave's customer three years ago, or Dave just doesn't want to hear from Chuck, or...? Sometime later in the meeting, Chuck again begins to speak and, again, barely makes a sound before Dave speaks up with great energy and enthusiasm. Again Chuck shuts up. Again he feels pinched. Again his ego and mind are at work, and he is getting angry. Later the same thing happens again, and again near the end of the meeting—four times in all.

By the end of the meeting, most people in Chuck's situation would have angrily built a Wall. Most, if they chose to confront Dave would do so in anger. They would have read Dave's mind to be certain of his motives. They would say something like, "Dave, you've cut me off! You are trying to impress the boss! You don't want me to say anything!" They might add epithets and unkind references to Dave's ancestry. Dave would naturally feel attacked, get defensive, and respond with something like, "You don't have anything worth saying anyway!" The conflict is now clearly destructive.

A common alternative—and more likely—would be for Chuck to leave the meeting hurt and angry, and with a private vow to avoid Dave forever more if at all possible. (Thus, Dave may never know how the Wall between him and Chuck was established).

If Chuck learned to describe behavior rather than attribute motives, the outcome of their experience might be radically different. Let's help Chuck examine what actually happened, what he observed, and what he can do with his observations to short-circuit trouble. What Chuck actually observed is that, four times during the four-hour meeting, he began to speak and, just as he did so, Dave spoke up and Chuck chose to stop speaking. That's all Chuck observed! To elaborate, an aware Chuck would observe the following sequence: (1) Chuck formulates his statement and begins to speak; (2) just as he begins to talk, Dave speaks; (3) Chuck *chooses* to stop talking; (4) his ego and mind go to work, search out reasons for Dave's action, and find a self-centered motive that Chuck attributes to Dave; (5) the event is repeated three more times, and each time, Chuck reinforces the attribution; and (6) Chuck acts on the attributed motive—as if he could read Dave's mind—by some form of either attack or avoidance.

If Chuck were to approach Dave by describing behavior, he might say, "Dave, four times during the meeting, when I started to say something, you spoke up and I shut up." That may be enough. However, under the right circumstances, he might add something like, "I'm fantasizing that you don't want to hear from me for a number of possible reasons." He might also add, "I'm feeling frustrated and angry." In other words, Chuck makes "I statements" describing only observed behaviors and, if appropriate, his reactions.

If Chuck did so—particularly with the full and honest realization of knowing nothing more about why Dave was behaving as he was, as an observer and not as a victim—Dave's response may very well be something like, "Oh, I'm sorry, I know I do that sometimes. We must be interested in the same issues. Please throw something at me if I ever do that again!" Instead of a destructive conflict, they now have a closer relationship. (Again, there are no panaceas. Some people in Dave's position would be offended and defensive no matter how skillfully Chuck presented the situation.)

Just as "pinchees" must be willing to express themselves, "pinchers" must listen. They must listen in an unusual way—for full understanding of the *pinchee's* point of view. Actually, of course, both must listen for understanding of the other's perspective and impressions. Such listening is truly rare. M. Scott Peck, in *The Road Less Traveled*,[44] defines such listening as an act of love. This is indeed a great challenge: people are not generally loving when they feel offended.

Failure to listen is so common that it sounds like a cliche. We cannot dismiss it as such, however, if we hope to manage conflict. Listening is simply, basically, and undoubtedly essential to any relationship. Yet, in spite of the fact that we are lifelong participants in myriad relationships of all sorts, truly being heard is an exceptional experience for most of us.

True listening is without judgement, preconceived notions, or desires to tell one's own story. Such a listener is fully present for us at the moment, does not judge what we say or who we are, and wants only to understand and empathize with us. Such unconditional listening is so helpful and so scarce that the only way some people experience it is to buy it by the hour from a psychotherapist. Listening, of the type I have attempted to describe, is fundamental to psychotherapy, as the late Carl Rogers[46] has so eloquently explained.

Open-Mindedness

The one thing that has become clearer to me in the course of my life is that keeping an open mind is of utmost importance. The right kind of openness is the most precious human possession.... We need to take a firm stand, but we also need to feel that we have not thus put our feet in shackles. Wherever we stand, we should stand free and unbiased and grow aware of the world.

Martin Buber[6]

When I conduct workshops in listening, one of the fundamental skills I teach is paraphrasing. The idea of paraphrasing—repeating back the other person's message in one's own words to check for understanding—is immediately obvious to most people. However, the act of paraphrasing is not simple, and most people are unable to accomplish it without practice. Of the many barriers to effective paraphrasing (a full discussion is beyond the scope of this book), and the one I encounter the most, particularly among professionals, is problem solving. They jump into a problem-solving, advice-giving mode before hearing the problem!

Why people fail to listen can be answered in many ways, but all the reasons relate to one central truth: listening is an act of caring. No amount of skill training will compensate for a lack of real interest in understanding and knowing the other person. Using the paraphrasing technique helps when one wants to listen, but otherwise becomes just another barrier. True listening is from the heart.

Think, for example, of your response to your child who bursts into the room crying and possibly hurt. You would do everything possible to hear from the child about what happened. Although you may not notice it at the time, you would be working very hard at the act of listening. You would paraphrase, question, and listen very carefully before responding. Hard work and real caring are what it takes to hear another person.

I believe failure to listen is the most significant and wide-spread problem in communicating. The impact of not listening effectively can be dramatic, even in everyday work situations. It kills relationships and stifles attempts at conflict resolution.

One of my first experiences as a third party facilitator, almost two decades ago, involved a striking example of the impact of not listening. I was asked by the president of a prominent high technology company

Suppose a man can convince me of error and bring home to me that I am mistaken in thought or act; I shall be glad to alter, for the truth is what I pursue, and no one was ever injured by the truth, whereas he is injured who continues in his own self-deception and ignorance.

Marcus Aurelius Antoninus[26]

to work with a department manager, Calvin, who reported to the president, and a section manager, Don, who reported to Calvin. Don had been engaged in a heated, conflict with Calvin. Finally, Don not only told him off in the most caustic manner, but reported the same to the president and quit. Don was a stellar performer and would take a major piece of business with him when he departed. The president asked them to try a conflict resolution session with me. Although both were skeptical, they agreed—they had nothing to lose.

We met in a conference room at 8:00 A.M. and began the meeting by having each prepare a list of what bugged him about the other. The lists were long. (The Wall between them was so high that they had been passing each other notes in staff meetings to avoid speaking!) They each included strongly worded statements to the effect that the other was an incompetent manager, a technical disaster, a rotten administrator, an impossible communicator, totally untrustworthy, and a lousy human being. After a priority setting exercise, I asked them to go to work on the issue they agreed was number one.

As they worked, a rather bizarre communication pattern became evident to me. When Calvin was speaking and Don attempted to say anything, Calvin would increase his volume and keep on talking; if Don persisted, Calvin would eventually arise from his chair and almost shout at Don. When Don finally got the floor, his response to Calvin's attempts to speak was the same! My job was to bring this dance to their attention, to make them aware of what they were doing.

I can't recall which of them realized it first. One of them woke up to what he was doing. In other words, he experienced a "Eureka!" or an "Aha!" He "caught himself in the act." He was shocked and amazed. Shortly thereafter, the other had the same realization, and he, too, was nonplused by his discovery. I then asked them how often they each listened to the other. Since both were scientists, I expected an analytical response, perhaps a percentage. I'll never forget what they said. "Never." I challenged them, suggesting that "never" was too extreme; certainly, I maintained,they must have listened sometimes. They were adamant—"Never!"

The realization that neither listened to the other was the clear turning point in their relationship. Don withdrew his resignation and we quickly resolved their entire list of problems, many of which simply dissolved in the light of the new information each acquired by listening to the other. With just a little follow-on assistance from me, they worked well together in the same roles for over 14 years until Calvin retired.

The most frequent missing link in conflict situations, in my experience, is the definition of the problem. As I have attempted to illustrate in some of the foregoing examples, the actual problem is most often not what the protagonists in a conflict believe it to be, especially if they have allowed a Wall to develop between them.

> *A problem adequately stated is a*
> *problem well on it's way to being solved.*
> *R. Buckminster Fuller*

Sometimes a Wall develops swiftly, so people have to be quick to prevent its progress. Such was the case with my first meeting with Amos, a noted organization development (OD) consultant. Almost two decades ago, shortly after changing careers from line manager to OD consultant, myself, I hired Amos to facilitate my second team building experience. Amos was one of the biggest names in the field. I was to be his co-trainer. We were to work with a top-level research group in the company I worked for.

Amos and I met for the first time at breakfast. I began to tell him of the group, the data I had gathered and the nature of our organization. As I spoke, I grew increasingly uncomfortable with Amos. I found myself growing irritated with him and telling myself that I could always hire another consultant. When I realized how I was reacting, I hesitantly told him what was happening.

With Amos' astute assistance, I came to realize that my growing animosity toward Amos derived from the difference in our communicating styles and from my projection of my sense of inadequacy. I had just entered into my new career in which Amos was an acknowledged expert. Deep within, I had doubts about the adequacy of my preparation for my new profession. I was doing virtually all the talking in my attempt to inform Amos as quickly and as thoroughly as I could. Amos listened with a benign expression on his face, saying very little. I looked at the almost blank face of this renowned expert and saw him as judging me and finding me professionally inadequate.

Ridding Yourself of Dogmatism

A good way of ridding yourself of certain kinds of dogmatism is to become aware of opinions held in social circles different from your own. . . . If you cannot travel, seek out people with whom you disagree, and read a newspaper belonging to a party that is not yours. If the people and the newspaper seem mad, perverse, and wicked, remind yourself that you seem so to them.

Bertrand Russell[49]

He wasn't judging. I was projecting. His natural style, as he pointed out, was to say little. (I was to realize later, and thereby join many others in appreciating, his marvelous ability to say just the right thing at just the right time.) He pointed out his appreciation for my relatively loquacious communication style and asked me to keep it up; he said it was perfect for giving him the information he needed as an outsider working with the group for the first time.

Had I not expressed my feelings and, with Amos, found their cause, I would have missed one of the most valued professional and personal relationships of my life. We worked together well—enjoyed lots of accomplishments and fun—for almost a decade until my dear friend's untimely death.

Very often, as was the case with Amos and me, the clear identification of the problem brings the solution in tow. However, this is not always the case; sometimes special action is required.

For example, in Calvin and Don's situation, where the problem was a total lack of listening, with my assistance the two practiced listening during the afternoon. However, before we broke up, they realized that they both faced a lifetime of not listening and wondered what to do when their third party wasn't present. They decided a hand signal was needed that either could use as a signal to stop the other from talking.

The idea was that when Calvin was talking and Don attempted to enter the conversation without success, he would raise a finger. Calvin would heed the signal and shut up. Don would do likewise. Once this agreement was made, they practiced with their pinkies until the end of the meeting. The signal worked well back on the job, and eventually, they no longer needed it.

Working on the expressed problem, rather than finding the true, underlying source of the conflict, results in much unnecessary frustration.

This frustration feeds the common belief that conflicts are usually caused by "personality problems" and other unchangeable factors and, therefore, attempts at resolution are futile. As we have noted, conflicts are indeed tough to deal with once the Wall is established, but certainly not impossible. Finding the true source is key.

In organizations, for instance, salary complaints are routine. Management typically wrestles with such complaints by conducting salary surveys to assess competitiveness and by negotiating increases if warranted. Often, however, the dissension fails to disappear. It does not disappear because salary complaints are rarely complaints about salary. They usually are an outward expression of deeper problems, often stemming from a sense of being unappreciated. In other words, salary complaints are a rational repository for feelings of insecurity, resentment about a lack of recognition, or an imbalance between positive and negative strokes.

For example, I was hired by a major electronics firm to manage a department that was losing lots of money. One of the problems in the department was a virtual rebellion by the 100 or so technicians. Their complaint was inadequate salaries in comparison with technicians in other electronic firms in the region. The company had responded to their complaints by conducting surveys, which showed the salaries to be as high or higher than those at the other companies. The technicians and management had reached an impasse, and technicians critical to the future success of the department were leaving.

I met with the technicians and listened to their complaints. In addition to gripes about salary, they were upset about their working conditions. Their laboratory, like most older facilities in the San Francisco Bay area, was built without air conditioning. They were crowded. During the summer, the lab was hot enough to exceed the temperature range for which some of the instruments were calibrated. They were responsible for critical measurements and tight deadlines. The underlying theme that began to emerge was "management doesn't care about us."

As their new manager, I obviously cared. The salary complaints began to diminish as I made my investigations. Their egos had translated the emotional "management doesn't love me, so I'm mad at them" into the rational "I'm not being paid what I'm worth." The entire problem was finally resolved by the addition of a few ordinary, electric fans in the lab!

Likewise, many arguments between family members about keeping rooms clean, taking out the garbage, spending too much money, coming home late, not helping with the yard, and so forth are indirect requests for reassurance and support. They are often some version of "I need to know you really love me" or sometimes just "I'm tired."

The list of problems leading to the erection of Walls between people is endless. Likewise, the solutions leading back to stability are without number. In my experience, they include specific, concrete actions such as changing the color of the house, new carpets, reorganizations, new office arrangements, revised goals and expectations, changes of title, changes in compensation, redistributions of work, contract changes, and on and on. They also include more nebulous and subjective solutions like changes of attitude, recognition of differences in personality, acceptance of different values, changes in interpersonal processes, and accommodation to unfamiliar management styles. In any case, they require commitment, persistence, patience, and good will.

And after all of that, the new state of stability will also be temporary.

An excellent way to finalize a conflict resolution process and to facilitate the reestablishment of stability is to make a deal. (Sometimes, little else is needed to get around the difference.) A deal consists of three elements:

1. What I want from you to be satisfied in our relationship and/or to get my job done is... .

2. What I'm willing to give you so you'll be satisfied in our relationship and/or so you'll get your job done is... .

3. How we'll track 1 and 2.

Each person makes his or her wants specific. Both formal (e.g., cost, schedule) and informal (e.g., social interaction) wants are included. The wants and gives are negotiated to everyone's satisfaction. Sometimes it helps communication to write them down.

Recognizing that even the clearest deal can't cover every contingency—that the unexpected will happen, that mistakes will be made, that anyone can have a bad day—step 3 is an agreement on what action will be taken when an apparent breach of the deal occurs. It is essentially a "don't gunnysack" agreement. The idea behind it is not to assume the worst and not to ignore the issue. The most frequent agreement here, in my experience, is simply to agree to get on the phone immediately and find out what is actually happening and to make whatever adjustments are required.

Figure 6 is a summarizing statement. Walls are prevented by keeping the stones from being set into place. The signal for action is the pinch. If a Wall develops and the relationship is valued, seek competent third party assistance. Within organizations, such assistance can sometimes be found within the human resource department or through an outside organization development consultant. For marital problems, seek out a topnotch psychotherapist experienced in dealing with such conflicts. With competent help, most Walls can be defeated one way or another, so don't give up too soon. Remember, the art of managing conflict to nurture rather than limit relationships is simple—not easy. It calls for your effort to establish mutual expectations at the outset of the relationship with the full understanding that the stability thereby created cannot last. This means that your viable, long-term relationships require nurturance. You and each of the other parties must take full responsibility for the relationship and take appropriate action at the first sign of trouble.

Taking action is facilitated by certain learnable skills, including direct, assertive expression, effective listening, description of feelings, description of behavior, and checking perceptions. Problem solving skills and insight into the nature of interpersonal problems help. Making a deal can make a real difference. A major requirement is caring more about the relationship than about being right. The most important asset of all is self-understanding.

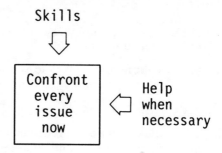

Figure 6. The Key to Effective Conflict Management

Moral: The skills required for conflict
management are simple, but
they rarely are acquired as part
of growing up. Learn them and
use them.

Studying the Adversary's Case

The greatest orator, save one, of antiquity, has left it on record that he always studied his adversary's case with as great, if not still greater, intensity than his own. What Cicero practiced as the means of forensic success requires to be imitated by all who study any subject in order to arrive at the truth. He who knows only his own side of the case knows little of that.

John Stuart Mill[41]

HOW TO LEARN CONFLICT MANAGEMENT SKILLS

Learn as though you would never be able to master it; hold it as though you would be in fear of losing it.
Confucius

The best way to learn conflict management skills within your organization is to work with a competent organization development consultant on your own real differences with others and/or on team building with your work group. For marital issues, you and your spouse can work with a qualified counselor or therapist.

The third best way is to take courses covering the subject. I've taught many. Most don't seem to have a significant long-term impact. A possible exception is U.C.L.A.'s Leadership and Human Relations Laboratories, now in its fourth decade.

Between the two in likely effectiveness is practice on your own with interested friends or colleagues. Although you can usually learn more working with a qualified consultant, most people have so much potential for improvement that personal practice can pay big dividends. The following are suggestions for practicing effective listening, checking perceptions, describing feelings, and expressing a difference. As your interest grows, you may derive other approaches from consulting your training staff, friends, counselors and/or the library. You may even invent your own.

Listening

The primary requirement for effective listening is *caring about what the other person has to say.* The importance of this requirement cannot be overemphasized, particularly since the last thing we may want to hear are

Understanding Opposing Views

It is important to learn not to be angry with opinions different from your own, but to set to work understanding how they come about. If, after you have understood them, they still seem false, you can then combat them much more effectually than if you had continued to be merely horrified.

Bertrand Russell[48]

the assertions of someone who is angry with us. If we care, we will attend to the other person: we will focus our full and undivided attention on understanding him or her. We will find a quiet, nondistracting environment where we can concentrate, face the other person with an open body stance, maintain eye contact, and lean forward to hear and observe every nuance and expression. To do this, we must recognize that effective listening is hard work. I find listening to be one of the most energy-draining aspects of my work.

Another primary requirement is self-understanding and awareness. The extent to which we listen effectively depends upon how well we know our own unique, personal barriers to the listening process. The following are some examples of common barriers that require self-awareness to overcome. (Since we tend to deceive ourselves, you may want to ask a friend or colleague for candid feedback.)

1. Discounting the entire message if you find even one flaw

2. Deciding from the sender's appearance and/or delivery style whether or not the message is worthwhile

3. Allowing your own biases on the subject to interfere with hearing the message

4. Listening selectively for what you want to hear or believe the other person will say

5. Responding before hearing the other's viewpoint

6. Allowing the status of the person to color the content of what you hear

7. Mentally rehearsing your response rather than paying full attention to what the sender is saying

8. Listening for agreement rather than understanding

9. Allowing your mind to wander

10. Having to be right, to win, or to have the last word

11. Filtering the other's message through your own judgments, "shoulds" and "shouldn'ts"

12. Being out of touch with your own feelings (so that you are unaware of the messages behind them)

13. Failing to use your eyes, as well as your ears, effectively

14. Getting a button pushed and seeking revenge or turning off

15. Not exercising sufficient empathy for the other person

16. Rejecting the other in any way

17. Responding in an unbalanced manner by suppressing or discounting your gut responses and intuition in favor of a demand for "logic" or "rationality."

A Listening Exercise

Here's a listening exercise you can try, preferably with two other people. Find a quiet place and identify a controversial subject to talk about. The controversial subject can be any issue about which the three of you disagree (or could disagree). You may have a real issue that is suitable; if not, find something you can argue emotionally. Good bets usually include politics, abortion, religion, child rearing, morality standards, and the like.

Specify the subject and decide which two of the participants will initially discuss it and which of you will act as observer. Make sure the two speakers take opposing views. Let them begin. If you've set this up right, the two will quickly become involved in a heated discussion. The observer is likely to see an increasing divergence of views and escalating conflict.

Once a level of heated conflict has been established, evoke the following rule to be enforced by the observer: before responding to the other person's remarks, you must (1) *reflect, feedback, and paraphrase the other's message,* and (2) *express your perception of the other's feelings.* When the exercise works well, the observer will be able to see these skills develop:

• Initially, people find paraphrasing very difficult to accomplish, and thus the observer may have to work hard to enforce the rule.

• As skill in paraphrasing is developed, the conversation will

Putting Ourselves in the Other's Place

To be charitable, we must put ourselves in everyone else's place—not to agree with everyone, but to understand his meaning and to allow him his due.

Karl Jaspers[18]

most likely converge and the tone shift from conflict toward conciliation.

- The reflection of feelings (perception checking) will tend to promote the description of feelings.

- The participants will be pleasantly surprised at the results.

The observer then reports his or her observations to the others and they discuss the experience. Each participant takes a turn as the observer and the exercise is complete.

Keep repeating the exercise, perhaps weekly, until sufficient comfort with paraphrasing, checking perceptions, and describing feelings is established. Then, each of you go out and apply your skills—shock and impress your spouses, kids, and coworkers!

We cannot account here for all of the possible directions and potholes evoked during this exercise. That's why an experienced consultant can make all the difference. However, experience has taught me some likely pitfalls and aids to progress, which I will present in no particular order:

1. It will help—particularly without the aid of a professional— to assume that *the sole judge of the accuracy of a paraphrase is the person sending the message.* He or she must agree with the paraphrase before the two can proceed. (How often people get into arguments about the accuracy of the paraphrase, itself! "But you said...!")

2. Generally, engineers, scientists, lawyers, business managers, and other problem solvers often fail to reflect correctly because they hear only part of the message, jump to a conclusion, and immediately proceed to solve the problem they have concluded exists. This leads only to confusion and further argument.

3. A major listening challenge stems from the fact that the brain is much quicker than the mouth. This leaves the listener with losts of opportunity to listen to his or her own mind rather than to the sender. If the receiver lacks confidence in his or

her ability to deliver a spontaneous response and/or must win the argument, he or she will mentally rehearse rather than hear. A helpful hint for this situation is for the listener to take brief notes of key ideas, then return full attention to the sender.

4. If you want to converge—in fact, if you want to get along with others—a good general rule is *do not make others wrong.* Remember that each person's views make sense to him or her and adopt a win-win attitude. Paraphrasing and coming to understand the other's view is greatly aided by such an orientation. This is especially true of perception checking; imagining yourself in the other's position will help you to understand his or her feelings.

5. A paraphrase is not parroting. Feed back *meanings,* not words.

6. A paraphrase can be a question—just make sure it is a question, not a statement in disguise. (Many people use questions as a way of making statements while shifting the responsibility to the other; e.g., "Do you mean you really don't love your mother.")

7. A skill of great impact and consequence in many circumstances, and a true test of the ability to listen, is the summarizing of the other's entire viewpoint or argument—both meanings and feelings—from his or her perspective. Sometimes it is extremely helpful to do so for major segments of a complex issue as it unfolds.

Remember that listening is simple, but not easy. Persistence and patience are often required.

Consider a brief example involving two acquaintances who meet on a bus on the way to work. The dialogue is necessarily simplified and condensed—thus perhaps a bit stilted—in order to bring forth and highlight the listening skills illustrated.

Speaker: Hi.

Listener: Hi, how are you?

Speaker: Uh...Okay...I guess....
(long silence)

Listener: I'm sure it's none of my business, but I can't help but notice that you seem troubled. Are you okay?

Speaker: Well, it's good of you to ask. I'm okay, I'm just a bit worried....

Listener: Worried? (said softly, with concern and full attention)

Speaker: Yes, my son, Johnny, is a new teacher and I'm afraid he won't do very well. (worried look, slightly shaky voice)

Listener: Oh, you're concerned about your son. I have kids and I know what it's like to worry about them.   *(perception check)*

Speaker: Yes, I am worried; I'm afraid he just won't make it.

Listener: I know that teaching jobs are scarce; can't he find work?   *(perception check)*

Speaker: Yes, he found work. He just got a job in a junior high school.

Listener: Oh, teaching in a junior high can be tough and the kids are a pain; don't you think he can handle it?   *(perception check)*

Speaker: Oh no, he can take care of the teaching okay and he gets along great with the students, but he has to share an apartment with several others and he won't be able to go out in the evening or get the car he's been wanting so much.

Listener: I think I'm beginning to understand. What you're saying is that you are concerned that Johnny is facing a lifestyle he won't like, and that it will impact his teaching. Is that it?   *(paraphrase)*

Speaker: Not so much his teaching directly, but that he'll be terribly unhappy.

Listener: Oh, so the problem is that Johnny's new job doesn't pay enough to support the way he likes to live?   *(paraphrase)*

Speaker: Right!

Listener: I see. I hope I understand what's troubling you. What I hear you saying is that Johnny has taken a job teaching in Junior High. You know he's good at his teaching and enjoys it; however, you

*You can only hope to find a lasting solution to a
conflict if you have learned to see the other objectively,
but, at the same time, to experience his difficulties
subjectively.*

Dag Hammarskjold[25]

---

don't believe he will make enough money
to support the lifestyle he likes, so
you're worried that his new career will
ultimately make him unhappy and that
he will have to find another path. Does
that about sum it up?   *(summarizing)*

Speaker: It sure does! It feels good to talk about
it and be understood. I'm glad I ran
into you today.

Listener: I hope everything works out for Johnny.

Speaker: Thank you.

Expressing a Difference

In the discussion of Chuck and Dave's situation, the skill of describing behavior was specified as key to expressing a pinch. "I statements" were also mentioned. The factor most likely to impede or block such skills is our tendency to judge others and ourselves. We do so more or less continuously, thereby blinding ourselves to the clear observation of behaviors.

Again, the best approach to developing these skills is working with a professional organization development consultant. A second best method for some people is assertiveness training. Check with your local educational institutions.

Another effective approach is to team with a friend or colleague who would also like to learn conflict management skills. Simply agree that each will give the other feedback whenever either is judgmental and to practice describing behavior and making I statements with each other.

Books on assertiveness[1] can help you and your partner(s) develop a self-help program to increase your ability to avoid building Walls between yourself and others.

Moral: Dedicating ourselves to learning and *practicing* the skills can result in major improvements in our relationships. This is particularly true of *listening*.

Accepting Otherness

To recognize and to accept the otherness of a person
means to respect him as a valuable being in his own
right, in his independence. This attitude is incongruous
with any idea of possessiveness or any tendency to
use him as means to an end, be this in the form of
exploitation, domination, possessiveness, or some other
attitude.

Andras Angyal[2]

C   H   A   **10**   P   T   E   R

THE ROLE OF CONFLICT MANAGEMENT IN ORGANIZATIONS

Conflict is the gadfly of thought. It stirs us to observation and memory. It instigates to invention. It shocks us out of sheeplike passivity, and sets us at noting and contriving...conflict is the sine qua non *of reflection and ingenuity.*

John Dewey

Besides the crucial role effective conflict management plays in interpersonal relations, it is pivotal in a broader sense to organizational effectiveness. Leadership, creativity, effective management, goal setting, planning, problem solving, teamwork, and organizational renewal all depend upon managing conflict for excellence. This list is arbitrary and could be expanded or broken down almost indefinitely. Because the need for effective conflict management permeates every facet of organizational life, we cannot detail every nuance of the subject. However, we can consider enough to recognize the all-too-frequent absence of the effective expression and working through of differences. We can start almost anywhere since all aspects of organizational life are interrelated.

We will begin with teamwork, the essence of effective organizations. One definitive element of teamwork is a common vision and common critical objectives. That seems obvious. Yet many organizations fall short of establishing true commonality because they suppress the conflict required. People usually need at least to ask questions—and receive candid answers—about where the organization is heading and where, specifically, they each fit. They want to be able to "buy into" the vision, but need to assure them-

Acceptance of Otherness

Genuine conversation, and therefore actual fulfillment
of relation between men, means acceptance of otherness.
When two men inform one another of their basically
different views about an object, each aiming to
convince the other of the rightness of his own way
of looking at the matter, everything depends so far
as human life is concerned on whether each thinks
of the other as he is, whether each, that is, with all
his desire to influence the other, nevertheless unreservedly
accepts and confirms him in his being this man and
in his being made in this particular way.

Martin Buber[7]

---

selves that their personal ambitions and values are in concert with it. Doing so may require expressing and working through differences.

If, as is so often the case, they are expected to "toe the line," "play the game," "not rock the boat," the organization achieves only a superficial sense of commonality that fails to energize and motivate. Without confronting differences, concerns, issues, trepidations, and uncertainties, people tend merely to go along without truly caring or feeling they have a personal stake in the success of the organization.

The requirements for confronting effectively here are essentially the same as those that intervene when a Wall begins between people. If the sense of belonging to a team has not been established, there is, in fact, a Wall between management or the organization and the employees. In this case, the employees will generally be reluctant to ask direct questions, particularly those related to personal career concerns. If they feel they will place themselves in jeopardy by expressing differences, they either won't express them, will find a way to do so indirectly (and, perhaps, destructively) or pretend to go along. In any case, motivation lies dormant and productivity suffers.

Likewise, the quality of the critical objectives or goals will suffer. A key to effective goals lies within the quality of the relationship between managers and nonmanagers.[38] If they can confront effectively, the quality of the goals will likely be as high as they can be under the circumstances. If they cannot, the goals may be meaningless.

I have been conducting team building sessions for all sorts of groups for almost two decades. My first step in the process is usually a private interview with each person wherein I ask them what's going well and what problems they experience.[10,14] I have run into the following situation at least once a year. Most of the participants tell me that the boss plays a game with them. They say he (all examples thus far have been males) calls the group together and tells them he wants to develop a set of key goals (variations of this feedback have included solving a problem or making a decision) *together*. They tell me they know the boss actually has his mind made up regarding the response he wants. Without realizing it, he has somehow conveyed the real message that differing with him is not truly acceptable. In other words, he has clearly conveyed a non-verbal demand for his desired outcome while verbally stating that he wants a participatory, even consensusual, decision.

When I ask the participants how they respond to his request for a joint effort, they tell me they play the game by discussing the matter for a while, then giving the boss the required response. They consider the whole process nonsense and resent it.

In contrast, the bosses all expressed their satisfaction and pleasure at having "a good team," at "giving my people a sense of participation," at "getting them to make the right decision and believe it's theirs," at "guiding them to the right objectives," and the like. One top manager, who I'll never forget, called it, "getting all the horses in the corral." So they believe.

Basic to the team building process is developing the group's ability to argue effectively. Thus, during the session, the boss in each case was confronted by the group members for the first time. In each instance, the boss was surprised to find how transparent were his real motives. Realizing the waste of energy and buildup of resentment resulting from their avoidance of conflict was a revelation to all.

Furthermore, once the group began to express and work through their differences and concerns, the increase in the quality of the objectives, goals, and decisions was usually dramatically obvious.

The creativity of groups is usually better than that of any individual member if the group is composed of people with different backgrounds, views, and styles, and if they feel free to express their differences. If they don't differ effectively, we have the all-too-familiar committee whose creativity is often even less than that of any of its members.

> *The value of dissent is not purely negative;*
> *it does more than protect us from error.*
> *It often points to the truth. One could*
> *make a good case for the proposition*
> *that the heros of science, the arts, and*
> *the professions have been dissenters.*
> *Carey McWilliams*

Being Present

When one has become fascinated by something—a problem, a person, a book, a scene—then the object of fascination fills a person's experience, and nothing else exists for him. This is the case, for example, in "true dialogue" between persons. The participants in dialogue are "fully there"—their thoughts are not preoccupied with unfinished business, or fantasy that is irrelevant to the ongoing conversation.

Sidney Jourard[22]

The stereotypical government bureaucracy (not all government agencies fit this stereotype) is perhaps the most obvious and public example of the consequences of a failure to support the expression of differences. Important decisions are made by the isolated (because subordinates won't risk differing with them) upper managers, often without their realizing they have done so. Since each of the junior bureaucrats carefully protects his or her own territory and is almost entirely oriented and reactive to directions from above, the buck is silently passed to the top. Creativity and motivation are stillborn in such environments. One of the consequences is the notorious inefficiency of many governmental operations.

Because all aspects of organizational life are interrelated, beginning with teamwork led us to the realization that effective dissent is required for a common vision, mutual goals, real motivation, and group innovation. If we have eliminated a common vision and key objectives, the motivation to collaborative to achieve the objectives and the ability to innovate, we also have thereby wiped out leadership. Nor can the organization effectively renew itself, since renewal requires confronting the old and creatively establishing new and better approaches.

One of the saddest and most directly debilitating consequences— to both the organization and individuals affected—of the lack of willingness to confront is the failure of most performance appraisal systems. A well done performance appraisal process is probably the best tool a manager has.[36] The systems are ineffectual primarily because most managers will not confront competently; they are uncomfortable doing so and lack the necessary skills.

Without the ability to express differences and manage conflict, they often can't generate meaningful goals and expectations (although they may believe otherwise). Thus, they don't develop worthwhile standards of performance. Whether or not they have such standards, they judge performance; yet, more often than not, they don't fully confront poor performance. Doing so is simply too uncomfortable, so they find ways to rationalize their avoidance. During the past quarter century, I have repeatedly observed the unfortunate, sometimes tragic, consequences of such avoidance:

1. Poor performance is tolerated, sometimes even masked. This directly limits the output of the organization and tends to demoralize good performers. Consequently, the business suffers.

2. Poor performers are given positive performance ratings, sometimes for decades, until business declines force them to be laid off. To justify the layoff, they receive their first negative appraisal prior to being released. Many are thereby almost psychologically incapacitated.

3. A variation of the above is the older employee who receives his or her first honest (and critical) appraisal, often from a new, young, dedicated manager. I have researched close to 50 such cases, and in each case, without exception, every previous manager recognized the problem and either didn't confront it or so carefully hinted at its existence that the employee failed to get the message. I contacted previous managers going back as far as 30 years. Thus, these employees learned of their limitations in their chosen career in their 50s instead of in their 20s or 30s when they would have had more options. Tragic.

4. My surveys of younger employees reveal that many believe their appraisals are too positive. They conclude that (a) the boss doesn't know enough about their work to assess their contribution accurately, and/or (b) the boss doesn't care enough to let them know their strengths and weaknesses so they can plan for development, and/or (c) the boss won't tell them. None of these deficiencies contribute to confidence, trust, loyalty, morale, or performance.

5. Many employees consider appraisals a kind of bad joke. Thus, the credibility of their managers suffers considerably in their eyes.

In other words, the lack of effective confrontation can turn the performance appraisal process, the organization's potentially most positive asset, into a pathetic liability (these days, even a legal liability).

The damage to organizations, and to the many of us who earn our way working in organizations, by the avoidance of confrontation is incalculable and enormous.

Helping to Clarify

*In every fruitful dialogue, each participant must help
the other to clarify his thought rather than to force
him to defend formulations about which he may
have his doubts.*

Erich Fromm[11]

The oil that lubricates the wheels of any organization is trust. Trust is built by trusting and by being trustworthy. Trusting means dealing with others openly, without manipulation or guile. It requires the willingness to be open, hence the courage and confidence to be vulnerable.

That which we know we come to trust.
Richard Beckhard

Being trustworthy primarily means keeping both the letter and the spirit of all deals and commitments and practicing the Golden Rule. Trustworthiness within organizations means that a commitment sealed by a word or a handshake is every bit as secure as any commitment by contract—usually, even more so.

Operating in an atmosphere of openness and trust requires caring and confrontation. Trust must be caringly nurtured and maintained. Since stability in relationships and situations—in life—never lasts, differences are bound to arise. Our caring then is manifested mainly by dealing with differences as they become evident. In other words, we must care enough and have the courage to confront if trust is to be kept alive.

When trust and openness are not the key characteristics of organizational life, we have the all-too-familiar "audit mentality" and the "mindless bureaucracy." The broader social order becomes that of the "litigation society." The costs are immense because of managers who can't delegate, "empire building," political maneuvering, redundant reporting, low morale, unnecessary stress, low creativity, lack of teamwork, protection of territory, poor communication, hidden conflicts, and so on. Attempts to legislate organizational effectiveness without confrontation are enormously costly: policies, procedures, rules, quality control, formal contracts, redundant reporting, audits and audits of audits—all reinforced by sanctions and the courts. Low trust and the lack of courage to confront to maintain trust lead to overburdened organizations that sink into a noncompetitive state.

The impact on individuals working in such organizations is both a cause and an effect of the lack of competitiveness, as well as a human

Listening with Understanding

Real communication occurs when we listen with
understanding. What does this mean? It means to
see the expressed idea and attitude from the other
person's point of view, to sense how it feels to him,
to achieve his frame of reference in regard to the
thing he is talking about.

Carl Rogers[46]

tragedy. The self-fulfilling prophecy is a major factor. Trust begets trust.
One of the most powerful means of empowering people toward the realization of their full potential is trust and acceptance—loving them as they are.

> *Trust men and they will be true to you;*
> *treat them greatly and they will show*
> *themselves great.*
>
> *Ralph Waldo Emerson*

When people are not trusted, particularly by those in power (managers, parents, governments), their behavior eventually tends to conform
to expectations. A real life example may clarify the process.

U.S. Government contractors are required to follow certain procurement rules based on the assumption that individuals can't be trusted
to keep the best interests of the government in mind. These rules include
complex competitive bidding processes and elaborate selection procedures.
Eleanor was Manager of Training and Development in such an organization
and an expert in her field. She was asked by management to provide a
course in sales for the managers of the company. She knew that the cheap-
est way to proceed would be to buy an off-the-shelf course from one of
the many possible vendors and tailor it to fit her organization. Eleanor
proceeded to review the available programs. After about a year of searching,
she found exactly the course she needed. She knew no other course would
do; however, she also knew that the key differences between the chosen
course and the dozens of others on the market would be difficult or impossible to explain to a government auditor. Because the course she wanted
was one of the more expensive courses available and she knew the procurement process would force her to purchase a cheaper and ineffective
course, Eleanor faced a dilemma. The system, because it assumed she
might be dishonest and discounted her expertise, was pushing her toward
untrustworthiness as a requirement for effectiveness. She had to beat the
system to produce a quality product at relatively low cost.

The alternatives she faced were as follows:

1. Follow the rules and deliver a poor product.

2. Avoid the procurement procedure by personally developing a course from scratch; in this way she could produce the required quality but at an enormous cost compared with modifying the purchased program.

3. Back in to the procurement cycle by developing an analytical decision-matrix that appeared to consider the alternate courses and justified the purchase of the chosen course.

4. Find a way to hide the purchase of the course.

In other words, although Eleanor is a cost-conscious, ethical expert, she cannot directly make the purchase that would be most effective and least expensive overall. The red tape she must wrestle with, because the system assumes her to be untrustworthy and her management unwilling to confront her decision, demoralizes Eleanor and requires her to, in effect, be untrustworthy to be effective. This is self-fulfilling prophecy in action—and it's an everyday occurrence.

The most debilitating effect of the avoidance of conflict on members of organizations is subtle, but we all know it from experience. We shrink. Another example will illustrate. Don joined his company, a high-technology firm, after graduating from college with a degree in engineering. He rose through the ranks during a 20-year period of organizational prosperity by his ability to grasp the big picture quickly, his talent for communication, his creativeness, his leadership skills, and his unusually positive relations with everyone. Perhaps most of all, he was respected for his willingness to speak out and confront issues whenever he disagreed with his boss or colleagues. He was a dynamic and positive force in the organization, reporting to the president, when hard times hit.

The president's response to the economic problems was—as unfortunately is typically the case—driven by fear. He initiated cutbacks and became intolerant of conflict, particularly of any opposition to his views. It was during this period, which lasted for several years, that a number of us who worked with Don began to wonder what was wrong with him. He was obviously losing his spark. He virtually stopped speaking up in meetings, his creativity seemed lost, he repeatedly failed to exercise leadership and often appeared somewhat confused.

His friends tried to help without success. We began to consider the possibility of troubles at home, alcohol, even drugs. People began to write him off as past his prime. Where once he was among the first consulted on almost any issue, people began to overlook him. Some began to

A Basic Rule for Dialogue

The next time you get into an argument with your wife, or your friend, or with a small group of friends, just stop the discussion for a moment and, for an experiment, institute this rule: Each person can speak up for himself only after *he has first restated the ideas and feelings of the previous speaker accurately and to that speaker's satisfaction.*

Carl Rogers and F. J. Roethlisberger[47]

wonder when the president would replace him. I personally tried everything I could think of including directly confronting Don with his deteriorating performance. Nothing—not even my "hard love"—had any impact. I gave up, too.

Then, something unusual took place that told me what had happened to Don. Because of his strategic planning experience, the president asked Don to lead a planning session for a small subsidiary in another town. Don asked me to facilitate. I agreed. The first meeting was a lot of fun and extraordinarily productive. I was vaguely aware that Don was behaving differently and assumed he was merely happy with the meeting.

The second session, held about a week later, also went very well. I was beginning to realize (Aha!) that Don was acting a lot like his old self. By the end of the third meeting, I was startled—I was working with the old Don in all his glory! He was there, in front of my face, just as he had been for most of the 20 years I'd known him—almost as if he had been resurrected from the dead.

I realized (Aha!) what had happened to my old friend. His *joie de vivre* and competence had been dimmed by the increasingly restrictive atmosphere created by the president. Simply speaking, it had become risky for Don to voice his disagreements and ideas, so he had stopped doing so. The out-of-town planning meeting, which was chaired by Don and attended by a small group who were comfortable with conflict and supportive of each other, was a safe environment. Don simply bloomed again!

Unfortunately, most organizations affect their employees much as the president did Don. Such organizations are unhealthy for the employees and far less productive and competitive than they could be. The suppression of constructive conflict in organizations is analogous to not servicing and maintaining an automobile; the car wears out quickly, its performance deteriorates, and it sooner or later breaks down. As it does so, it's not much fun to drive.

Wrestling with the problems and dilemmas of everyday organizational life *requires* the ability to manage conflict. I can't recall a single situation in the past 20 years in which I was called to help resolve a conflict between individuals or groups or to facilitate a team building process where the people involved understood their problem. (No wonder they couldn't solve it!) Furthermore, after talking candidly with each person involved, I would not know the problem either. We could discover the problem only by working together—it would seem to emerge out of the center of the room—*as a result of expressing and working through the differences, past and present.* Without effective confrontation, many problems remain undefined, much less resolved. Since much of management is problem solving, managers must be able to produce a team that deals skillfully with differences, otherwise that manager's real power to manage is limited.

Without effective conflict management, the trust that glues the organization together and oils the operation does not develop. In its absence, the organization limps along and fails to achieve the ranks of the excellent. I believe that conflict management is the number one issue in the workplace today.

Moral: The management of conflict is absolutely essential to the effectiveness and competitiveness of organizations. The lack of proficient conflict management has a pervasive, detrimental impact on productivity and career fulfillment. Well managed conflict is a key to creativity, communication and goal achievement. It is required for the establishment and maintenance of trust, which is both the glue that holds teams together and the oil that facilitates their functioning.

III
P A R T

CONFRONTING OURSELVES

The Beauty of Genuine Dialogue

When unity of self and other is experienced and communication reaches a heightened personal meaning, life is being lived at a peak level. At times it seems unbelievable, almost beyond reach, but when it happens it is something of awesome beauty.

Clark Moustakas[42]

Most conflicts with others extend from conflicts within ourselves. Thus very often, more permanent and powerful means of precluding and resolving destructive conflicts stem from self-confrontation than from confronting others. Doing both can be particularly effective.

Conflict in One's Own Soul

A man should himself realize that conflict situations between himself and others are nothing but the effects of conflict situations in his own soul; then he should try to overcome this inner conflict, so that afterwards he may go out to his fellow men and enter into new, transformed relationships with them.

Martin Buber[5]

11
C　　H　　A　　P　　T　　E　　R

CONFLICT RESOLUTION WITHOUT CONFRONTATION

Sticks and stones will break my bones, but names will never hurt me!

Childhood rhyme

I was recently asked by Lois and Jenny, two managers in the hotel and conference business, to help them overcome their five-year old conflict. We met first thing in the morning. Only one hour after we began, we were successfully finished *without any interpersonal work between the two.*

We were able to accomplish this almost instant cure because of Lois' extraordinary level of self-understanding and Jenny's supportiveness. Jenny, the senior of the two managers, made some opening observations about Lois: her tendency to flare unpredictably, her defensiveness, her win-lose orientation, and the lack of trust in her by various coworkers. While Jenny sat and listened (remarkably!) without judging, we were able to establish that the core of the problem was Lois' passionate, personal commitment to excellence coupled with an underlying severe lack of self-esteem.

Lois quickly realized that she was an "offensive player" with a strong need to be right. Her desire for control, her driving need to win, and her basic distrust of others were causing her trouble. She wouldn't delegate; she fought aggressively, thus creating enemies; and because she was uncomfortable expressing her true feelings, she often sent "double messages," generating distrust. Once these issues were clarified and acknowledged, we quickly developed a strategy for getting Lois supportive feedback so she could be aware of her destructive behaviors as they took place. She's now well on her way out of her problems.

Consider another situation. A top manager of an organization presented me with a problem involving the manager of a project engineering

The Crucial Realization

*By our contradiction, our lie, we foster conflict
situations and give them power over us until they
enslave us. From here, there is no way out but by
the crucial realization: Everything depends on myself
and the crucial decision: I will straighten myself out.*
                                        Martin Buber[5]

unit reporting to him. I had known the project manager for a long time.
I experienced her as an analytical, rational, "left-brained," no-nonsense
kind of person. I had not seen her for several years. The top manager
said that he had received inputs from other managers throughout the company to the effect that she was arrogant, hard to get along with, and mis-
trusted. A few just said she was "a bitch." He asked me to work with
her. She agreed.

When I visited her to discuss the situation, it quickly became
apparent to me that she had done some sort of personal growth work
since I had last seen her. After three decades of intensive personal growth
experience, I can usually spot the signs. When I expressed interest, she
told me about the personal growth trainings she had taken.

As we turned from her personal growth experiences into the subject
at hand, she spoke with contempt of the lack of awareness of her fellow
managers. She referred to them as "fools" and said, "I don't suffer fools
lightly." Her tone conveyed bitterness and contempt. By asking a series
of leading questions, I was then able to help her become aware of the
likely impact of her contempt on the other managers. Her "Aha" was two-
fold: (1) she saw that she was judging the others harshly and in a manner
her personal growth training presumably had allowed her to transcend,
and (2) the reaction she was bound to trigger in others was self-fulling
and destructive of important organizational relationships. She was essentially on a self-defeating ego trip.

Her awakening sent her on a fence-mending mission throughout
the network of her organizational relationships. Her boss soon stopped
hearing complaints about her.

One more example. Many years ago, I was hired to manage a training and development organization. The previous manager had retired and,
rather than promote from within, the company searched outside for a new
manager. The apparent successor, Sal, was passed over. He was under-
standably unhappy. He asked me why he had not been given the job. I

We Must Realize Our Situation

You do not realize your own situation. You are in prison. All you can wish for, if you are a sensible man, is to escape. But how to escape?...If a man is at any time to have a chance of escape, then he must first of all realize that he is in prison. So long as he fails to realize this, so long as he thinks he is free, he has no chance whatsoever.

Gurdjieff[40]

THE BASICS, HOW WE COME TO UNDERSTAND OUR OWN REALITY

For practical purposes we have agreed that sanity consists in sharing the hallucinations of our neighbors.

Evelyn Underhill

We each create our own separate reality. One way we do so is by selecting what we experience. We can effectively pay attention to only one thing at a time. So, we turn down the car radio when we look to find the number of the house we've never visited; we turn off the television while we memorize a poem. We cannot hold a conversation and read at the same time.

We pick out what we choose to be aware of from an ocean of possibilities. If you are on the road and hungry, you see restaurants and little else; if you break off the heel of your shoe, the shoe repair shop stands out and the rest of your surroundings (including the restaurants) fade into the background. If you perceive so-and-so to be untrustworthy, you notice only evidence that agrees with your perception. You somehow hear just your own name from across a noisy room. Modern psychologists associate this process with the brain's "reticular activating system." Yogis, who for centuries have investigated from inside how the mind works, call it "desiring." We see what we want or desire to see, we choose what we are aware of—sometimes whether or not it's there.

Not only do we select what we experience, much of it is a product of our imagination. Suppose, for example, I draw your attention to a black horse about a hundred yards away. What you'd actually experience at that distance would be the sight of a two-dimensional black shape. That's all.

Each is Furthest from Himself

*We are unknown to ourselves, we men of knowledge—
and with good reason. We have never sought
ourselves—how could it happen that we should ever
find ourselves?...So we are necessarily strangers to
ourselves, we do not comprehend ourselves, we have
to misunderstand ourselves, for us the law "Each is
furthest from himself" applies to all eternity—we are
not "men of knowledge" with respect to ourselves.*
Friedrich Nietzsche[24]

Yet because of the nature of the mind, you would "see" something more: your own idea or concept of the horse. For example, how would you know the shape is a horse and not a cow or an elephant? That information is supplied by your mind. You would "see" the horse as three-dimensional, furry, warm, capable of neighing, and so on. Virtually all of what you experience as the horse actually is a creation of your mind! Further, our creations can be different. Suppose, for example, that you had recently been kicked and bitten by just such a horse, whereas I'd been raised with an affectionate horse who looked just like it. My horse would be a warm friend; yours might be a fearsome enemy.

Each of us creates our own horse. Likewise, we create everything and everyone we see. We create our own separate worlds largely from the contents of our own minds—from our personal, idiosyncratic databanks.

Since each of us has created our own world, no one else can be held responsible or accountable for our lives—for our happiness and success, unhappiness and failure. In particular, no one else is responsible for our conflicts. People are invariably responding in a way that makes sense *in their world.* Many of our conflicts are analogous to arguing with a fish over whether it's better to live on land or in water. The fish is right and so are we!

Once we see how our consciousness works, we realize that to truly know and experience what is, rather than the mind's illusions, requires the cessation of thought. (This will not sound so strange if you note that total concentration on anything—like full attention to what someone is saying—is possible only in the absence of thought.) Unless we somehow find our way around our own minds, our respective worlds will be cut mainly from the fabric of our own thoughts. Since our worlds are largely a creation of our thoughts, they are all different. No wonder communication is so difficult and misunderstanding so frequent!

We also obscure our contact with what is and contribute to our false creations by projecting, as discussed in Chapter 7.

Even the way we define or create ourselves as human beings is arbitrary and misleading. Suppose you are looking at me. The boundary between myself and the air around me or the chair I'm sitting on would be clear to you. What's Dick and what's not Dick would seem obvious. Actually, it's anything but obvious. If we could sufficiently magnify the boundary where my ear meets the air, we all know we'd see molecules and atoms and that we would be hard pressed to distinguish me from the air.

Suppose the sun went away? How long would you or I last? Suppose the atmosphere, the air we breathe, disappeared? What if the earth vanished? Suppose there was no more water anywhere? What if the whole food chain, from green plants to animals, vanished? Any of these events would have about the same impact as losing one's heart or lungs. We'd be dead and gone. Yet we don't define ourselves accordingly. Doing so would be much more realistic, much less misleading. Alan Watts, the great philosopher, said that we put a grid on the world to help us understand it and then we confuse the grid with the world.*

Perhaps your most important mental creation—and the one contributing most to trouble and conflicts—is your personal sense of identity, the "you" you think you are, your self-image or ego. My ego is my image of self-importance, my illusion of separateness, my myth of uniqueness, my false identification with that which is not truly me, my false identity. I'm using the term "ego" in the ordinary way most folks do. We talk of enhancing the ego. In organizations we deal with "status" and "recognition."

Most of us spend our lives trying in vain to satisfy the demands of our egos, living more or less constantly in a state of quiet desperation. The ego is an impossible taskmaster because we can't satisfy it. My ego compares me with others and, even if I'm "the best" now, sooner or later someone who is "better" will come along and I'll crash. Worse, maybe my ego compares me with what Karen Horney called my "idealized self-image,"[15] an impossible standard of perfection formed in early childhood. I always fall short, somehow, so I'm never quite okay. I remain vulnerable to any suggestion that I'm "wrong" or not "perfect."

Anything you lose that makes you feel less okay, desirable, or important is probably part of your ego. If the loss of your job, your title, your house, your car, your friend, your youth, or your looks would make you feel somehow less worthwhile, then they are just part of your ego. They are not you.

---

*Alan Watts published at least 26 books. Among the best known are: *The Wisdom of Insecurity* (1951); *The Way of Zen* (1957); *Nature, Man and Woman* (1958); *Psychotherapy East and West* (1961); *The Book: On the Taboo Against Knowing Who You Are* (1966); *In My Own Way* (1972); *Cloud Hidden, Whereabouts Unknown* (1973).

On Knowing Oneself

One must know oneself before knowing anything else.
It is only after a man has thus understood himself
inwardly and has thus seen his way, that life acquires
peace and significance.

Søren Kierkegaard[4]

We are not our minds, bodies, possessions, prizes, or positions. When we realize that, when it becomes fact for us, when we catch on to who we truly are, we will no longer believe we have to look into the eyes of others to see whether we're okay. We'll just know. And we'll know true peace, freedom, and love—and little or no conflict of a negative nature.

Our culture promotes enhancement of the ego, improvement of one's "self-image" or "self-concept." Note that even the ordinary terms, "image" and "concept," denote the unreal. It's a mass illusion, part of what Tart calls the "consensus trance."[53]

The truth is that the ego is our enemy. It may ultimately be our only enemy. This is a difficult point to argue on paper because the ego is considered "normal" and because the mind or intellect can't recognize the truth of the matter. The mind only knows perceptions, ideas, concepts, models, thoughts, and words. What is, the Truth, must be experienced directly. The mind and the ego work so closely together that they are sometimes referred to together as ego-mind.

A digression might help. Life must remain a mystery to the mind. Life can't be understood mentally. The attempt is something like trying to experience flying by playing with a toy airplane. Life can only be experienced directly. Psychology, sociology, philosophy, theology, and the other "ologies" and "isms" can be studied, intellectually understood, and argued. You can get Ph.D.s in each of these; you can't get corresponding certification in you, people, reality, or God. These cannot be explained or argued. They can be discovered. Within is the way.

> *One learns peoples through the heart,*
> *not the eyes or the intellect.*
> *Mark Twain*

Since I am not my body, thoughts, feelings or dreams, my mind can't conceive of who I truly am. So, my mind creates a self-image, a false me (my ego) and defends it ardently to avoid facing the disquieting vacuum of knowledge behind the false front.

On Self-Knowledge

After you get over the pain, eventually self-knowledge is a very nice thing. It feels good to know about something rather than to wonder about it, to speculate about it.

Abraham Maslow[32]

The mind thereby also creates a wellspring of destructive conflicts, because what comes with this false identity is the continual need to be on guard to defend it. The energy we expend defending this false self could be spent experiencing our lives.

What also comes with our false identities is comparison with the false identities of others and the resulting pervasive sense of inadequacy. It's phoney. Inside, the real me softly smiles, knowing without the possibility of doubt or error that I am completely okay and safe at home.

Sages throughout history have said that our actual identity is a consciousness beyond ego and mind. They tell us there is nothing to add and nothing that can be taken away. We are actually perfect as we are. Ego's illusion of separateness, image of self-importance, myth of uniqueness, and identification with the body, personality, possessions, and positions are all false. The mind's thoughts and feelings are just fantasy. All of these change constantly. There is a you, a center of consciousness, a self that stays calm and clear through all of these changes—a sense of self beyond mental understanding that can observe all of these variations and wisely choose the directions of your life.

The great writings of all places and times point out that our bodies, and all the trappings that come with them, are like vehicles that we drive through life. We can only do a good job of controlling them if we're clear about who we are and what it takes to steer. Until we are reasonably clear about our true identities, ego-mind will continue in the driver's seat and take us for a rough ride.

We can't discover our true identities without looking inside. We must look inside from inside, directly and experientially, not from outside through the distortion and limitation of definitions, theories, and models. That's what the Buddhists mean when they say that if we meet the Buddha we should kill him. We eventually must somehow drop all ideas, all thoughts, if we are to know ourselves. Thoughts are like the ripples on the surface of the water that keep us from seeing the bottom. Any "ism" or "ology," certainly including psychology, eventually must hinder or prevent our full awareness of who we truly are.

The "who I am," my true self, my center, or as close as I've been to being there, is a wonderful experience.[52] It is for you and for everyone else as well. The feeling—how can I describe it?—is lightness, peacefulness, confidence, being okay, clarity, creativeness, positivity, fulfillment, gratitude. This is our natural state, within us all the time. Consider a beautiful plant that needs sunshine, weeding, perhaps spraying, and a bit of the right food to grow to its full potential. Its potential is always present, although it can be hidden from view. The gardener's job is to lovingly remove the impediments so that it can grow and blossom into the fulfillment of nature's design. It is the same with us. We are nature, too. The entire flower is potentially in the seed. All that I am is within me, waiting to be realized. And the more I realize of it, the less I will find to argue about.

Moral: We truly create our own respective realities, largely by the almost independent actions of our minds. What we collectively call "reality" is largely a consensus shaped by our culture. The aspect of this manufactured sense of what's real that probably contributes most to our needless conflicts is our self-image or ego. Getting out from under the domination of ego-mind frees us from vulnerability and opens us to the confidence of our true selves; we thereby awaken to a genuine understanding of others— and to life.

Becoming One With Yourself

Plato considered that man was himself only when he had become one with himself, only when he did not contradict himself. He saw it as man's greatest calamity to be at variance with himself, always changing his opinions and personality, inconsistent, whirled around by chance.

Karl Jaspers[21]

THE WITNESS

Hide not Thyself from Thine own self.
Isaiah 58:7

For me to discover who I am is for me to discover the reality of life itself. It's not easy to do. A great deal of illusion stands in the way.

Recognizing the following may help you get closer to reality, to your actual identity. When a friend asks what you are thinking about, you probably don't consider the question unusual and respond easily. To be asked how you are feeling is also an ordinary question. Again, you can readily share that information. It's ordinary, too, for any of us to discuss our bodies or some part of them: "I have to take better care of my body," "My skin is dry," "My head hurts," "I'm going to cut my fingernails." Likewise, describing one's dreams to a friend is anything but unusual. In other words, when someone asks you about your thoughts, your feelings, your body, or your dreams, you can readily respond if you wish to do so.

Notice carefully: who is the "you" I'm talking with? When you use such ordinary phrases as "my mind," "my body," "my thoughts," "my personality," "my feelings," "my dreams," "my nose," who is the "I" that has the "my"? Obviously, the "I" is not the mind, body, thoughts, feelings, or dreams. You are obviously none of these; you *have* them, just as our everyday language says.

I'm clearly talking with a part of you that can witness or observe, at least to some extent, all of the other. The ancient yogis called this central consciousness in each of us "the witness" or "the observer." A colleague dubbed it "The Chairman of the Board." It's so ordinary that it escapes our attention until we become conscious of being conscious, aware of being aware. From this state of witness consciousness, we observe—without judging—our thoughts, feelings, behaviors, and dreams. (Note that the witness is always awake.)

Please don't take my word for this. Just notice that it's a fact. When you get in touch with your own witness or observer, you will have the key to yourself.

The turning point in the process of growing up is when you discover the core of strength within you that survives all hurt.

Max Lerner

How to Witness

The act of witnessing demands that we get in touch with that essential and basic aspect of ourselves that *is* the witness. To do so, it will be helpful to notice how our insides operate. The best model I know is the psychosynthesis model.[3] Psychosynthesis tells us that we have any number of "subpersonalities" that can operate more or less independently. At any instant, we may be thinking, operating, and expressing ourselves through one of these subpersonalities.

Before you begin to think I'm describing something exotic rather than ordinary, consider what goes on in you when you are faced with a major decision. You will be carrying on an inner conversation between your subpersonalities, some of whom will be in conflict. As an example, let's tune in to what could be going on in Laura's mind as she contemplates buying an expensive, new sports car. Please feel free to change the names I have arbitrarily given to her subpersonalities. The issue facing Laura is whether or not to buy the car.

Subpersonality	Argument
Nurturing Parent:	*You deserve it; you've worked hard.*
Ms. Practical:	*You could fix up the old car and make it last another 5 years for only a couple of thousand dollars. $20K is too much for a new car and they depreciate so fast.*
Showboat:	*Boy, would I look good and be admired in that new car!*
Business Woman:	*That new car would make a great impression on customers.*
Mystic:	*You worry entirely too much about material things.*
Playgirl:	*Life is short; go for it!*
Not OK Child:	*That car is really too good for me— leather seats in my neighborhood?*

The Judge:	*You shouldn't want a car like that one; what's wrong with you?*
OK Child:	*Oooh, won't that red car be fun!*
Worry Wart:	*That new car will probably be stolen, at least the stereo and the wheels. Besides, another gas shortage is likely in the near future. And they may not honor the guarantee.*
Technical Self:	*Dual overhead cams, four valves per cylinder, turbocharged, independent rear suspension, series V-tires, 0.30 Cd streamlining, four wheel disc brakes, 0-60 in 7.5 seconds, .80g on the skid pad, 100 watt stereo, full analog instrumentation, 200 HP from 2.8 liters, reclining seats— terrific!*
Rationalizer:	*The old heap needs a new transmission, the paint is chipped and it'll need new tires soon— so it's time for a new car.*

Familiar, I'll bet. Familiar to me. Which me? The "me" who can notice all that's going on—the witness.

Lots of people who attempt to witness consciously for the first time instead actually get in touch with what I call "the Judge" in themselves. The Judge does not witness. A witness observes and reports without judgment. The Judge labels the observations as good or bad in some sense. Thus, since most of us experience an "Oh yuck" aspect to our Ahas, the Judge punishes us for making our discoveries. In other words, if the Judge in me labels what I discover negatively—e.g., "if you were more mature, you wouldn't feel that way!"—and I accept the judgment, I am punished for the discovery. Another way of saying this is that I am negatively reinforcing my self-realization. My crummy reward will be to stop facing myself and the painful joys of waking up.

The trick in dealing with the Judge, as with any other aspect of ourselves, is to witness the judgment rather than getting caught up in it—and then move on. Treat it as you would any other aspect of the ego. Some people find it helpful to thank their Judge as a means of releasing it.

One teacher I met labeled the Judge "El Protecto" and pointed out that it sometimes performs a protective function that is highly limiting. For example, if Marion considered confronting her boss, her El Protecto would tell her of the dangers of doing so and perhaps predict that she would be fired as a result. By witnessing and hence being clear about where the warning was coming from, Marion could choose whether or not to go ahead and how. She might thank El Protecto for the advice as a means of acknowledgment and release. Try it.

Witnessing is experiencing, not merely "thinking about." We experience and consciously take note of our thoughts, feelings, emotions, and intuitions. This point is worth emphasizing because of our tendency to believe that we understand something when we can give it a name. For example, if I knew nothing about the shiny, round, red object in my hand, calling it an "apple" would add nothing. But science has gone before me, so now that I can name it, I can go to the library and collect lots of intellectual information about it: what it is, how it grows, how to manage an orchard, and so on. What I will have then are lots of thoughts about the object in my hand. I might even study enough to conduct courses on the subject. I could perhaps even become a Professor of Theoretical Apple Science.

Would the professor then know his apples? Of course not. He would know only ideas about something labeled "apples," some of which could be applied, for example, to their efficient production. How much more can I experience if I witness my reactions to the object in my hand...?

I feel its weight pressing on my palm and the slight muscle tension in my arm required to hold it up to view. I note the waxy texture of its skin. I can smell its fragrance and marvel at its colors. I can hold it against my cheek and feel its coolness. I become aware of how delighted I am with this object and its beauty. And, the greatest joy of all, I can bite into it, hear the crack of my teeth breaking its skin and experience its marvelous, sweet taste!

I cannot transfer any of this knowledge to anyone else. They have to experience the apple for themselves, just as I have, and their experience may be different—they may not like the taste, for example. I'll never truly know their experience just as they can't experience mine. (When they say, "It tastes like an apple," are they experiencing the same taste as I do? I'll never know.)

Witnessing is not thinking about or analyzing. If I think about apples as I hold the object in my hand, I'll witness myself thinking, not having the other experiences. In fact, I can't have the other experiences if I'm thinking about anything. That's how it is when I witness myself; I taste the apple of myself and observe all of my reactions as objectively as I can. I am curious, intensely interested, and ready to experience what is.

Keeping a journal or notebook is an ancient technique that can materially assist the witnessing process. Taking time at the end of the day to write down our reactions—thoughts, feelings, body sensations—particularly when we have negative experiences, can be invaluable. Noting, for example, what triggers anger, depression, or worry every time it occurs can record a pattern of responses sometimes enabling us to be our own psychotherapists: "Wow, (Aha!) every time my boss gets that look on her face I briefly panic inside—just as I did when my mother disapproved of me. Isn't that something!"

Useful, also, when learning to observe ourselves, is not to take the process too seriously. A light, alert touch works best. We can't force Ahas; they come in their own time as "glimpses and glimmers."[50] When they arrive, we accept them as gifts. In between, we keep as alert as we can, write in our journals, and await the next discovery.

> *And what is it that makes most of us angry?*
> *Usually it's when someone has shown a*
> *lack of respect for us. The image we*
> *have of ourselves has been offended. So,*
> *conceited souls that we are, we get furious.*
> *Instead, we should simply be curious.*
> Soundings, *Vol. D, No. 1*

Moral: There is a part of each of us—close to our true identity—that has been called by many names throughout the millennia. Its ancient and descriptive yogic name is "the witness." Getting in touch with the witness, becoming aware that we are aware, is required for personal growth. It is so obvious that most of us overlook this central aspect of ourselves until it is pointed out to us.

Unmasking the Self

Veils cover our eyes, obstructing and distorting our view of reality. Similar veils obstruct our perception of ourselves, our self-image, thus distorting and darkening awareness of our true nature or identity. Carl Jung's psychology speaks of this artificial, illusory self-concept as the *persona:* this is the mask we manufacture for the sake of appearances, a kind of "cover" identity that hides our actual Self. The *persona* was actually the mask used by Roman actors to speak through as they acted their roles, and *persona* is the basis of our word *personality.* This suggests that personality, or ego, is a kind of cover, or mask, and that the "real" individual is hidden beneath.

Ralph Metzner[40]

14

C   H   A   P   T   E   R

WITNESSING

*Your inner Reality, your innermost Consciousness,
which is constantly watching the mind, is different
from the mind. Let the mind think whatever it likes.
At the same time be aware that you are not the
mind, you are only the witness of the mind; you
are the observer, the spectator, who is watching the
mind move. Knowledge is only another name for
right understanding of the mind. When our mind
becomes agitated or turbulent, we should not think
that we have become agitated or turbulent. We should
be able to watch our turbulence or our agitation
from a distance and see the endless creations of
the mind.*

Muktananda

Most importantly, witness how your mind works. You have
little or no control over it. Your mind has a will of its own. It generates
thoughts, images, and corresponding feelings whether you want it to or
not. If you doubt this, see whether you can avoid thinking of a pink monkey
for the next minute. Try it; it's an ancient demonstration of the mind's
independence.

Notice how your mind influences your daily life. What happens
when, for example, your loved one is overdue? Your mind plays disaster
films. Much like the old Saturday matinee serials, it quickly runs through
scenario after scenario, each more awful than the last. The same kind
of thing happens when someone gives you a "dirty look." Your mind builds
images out of all the imperfections, shortcomings, and inadequacies you
imagine of yourself.

The trouble is that we identify with these images instead of just
recognizing them as stuff of the mind. By identifying with them, we further
energize them. If, instead, we detach ourselves and merely observe them,

*Our sages say: "Seek peace in your own place." You
cannot find peace anywhere save in your own self...
When a man has made peace with himself, he will
be able to make peace in the whole world.*

Martin Buber[5]

they gradually subside of their own accord and leave us closer to the peace
of what is.

> *Most of the shadows of this life are caused
> by our standing in our own sunshine.*
> *Ralph Waldo Emerson*

When ego gets into the act, it works with the mind in a way that
seeds many conflicts. Suppose, for example, that part of Jake's self-image
is being a competent professional. Jake has pride in his work, his stature
as a professional, his credentials, and his reputation. If his pride is strong—
and our culture promotes such pride—Jake's coworkers might say he has
a big ego. Although often viewed as an asset, his big ego makes Jake vain
and vulnerable. His vulnerability might manifest something like this: Jake
writes or says something from the storehouse of his expertise; someone,
perhaps his boss, is unimpressed; Jake gets angry. From this point, many
pathways could lead to a Wall between them.

Something like the following has taken place. Jake speaks as an
expert, probably expecting to impress his boss. His boss responds in an
unexpected (to Jake) fashion: perhaps she ignores Jake or dismisses what
Jake has to say as unimportant. She may give Jake a condescending look
or even reject Jake's observations or recommendations. Jake would note
the response and compare it with his stored expectations. His ego-mind
would generate reasons and motives from his own stored repertoire of
possibilities.

One of the motives Jake's ego-mind is likely to offer is something
to the effect that his boss does not consider him an expert professional.
This would be a reflection of Jake's ego standards and true, underlying
sense of inadequacy. His response to his own thoughts would probably
be a fleeting sense of fear quickly covered by anger and perhaps followed
by depression. If he chooses not to lash out or try to make his boss wrong,
as many would do, he will probably harbor a sense of resentment that
eventually could lead to the building of a Wall.

Jake could circumvent the Wall building process by checking his perceptions with his boss (who may simply have suffered a gas pain). Jake could also consider the episode as an opportunity for growth rather than conflict. He could witness his own reaction to his boss's response and ask himself what makes him so vulnerable to it. "What is there about me that makes me react so strongly and emotionally to my boss's response?"

The answers to such questions, unfortunately, do not come easily. With sufficient self-understanding, the answer may not even be necessary. Following are a few of the infinite array of possibilities.

1. Jake could get in touch with, witness, and examine his own thinking. His thoughts are likely to be distorted by his ego. One common distortion would be thinking that his boss's rejection of an idea means his boss considers Jake incompetent. Burns[9] presents a particularly illuminating discussion of how we distort our thinking, thereby inducing anger and depression in ourselves.

2. Jake may be putting his parent's (father's or mother's) face on his boss. I suspect this sort of thing happens frequently in manager-subordinate conflicts—the boss/subordinate relationship follows a parent/child archetype—but seldom can one mention, much less verify, it. By witnessing his responses, Jake may have an Aha! telling him he is experiencing his boss as a parent figure. I recall one intense conflict resolution session between a brilliant supervisor and her boss, both of whom had realized considerable self-awareness and growth through psychotherapy. It eventually became vividly clear that the source of their long-running conflict was that the supervisor was reacting to her boss as she had to her mother.

3. Jake could, if he possessed the necessary awareness, confidence, and skill, find the state of consciousness within himself that could empathize with his boss.[53] He might thereby close the gap between his perceptions and those of his boss and enter into an appropriate, problem-solving discussion.

   During a team building session I facilitated several years ago, a secretary complained bitterly about the use of a table that sat in front of her desk. My first reaction (which I kept to myself) was to be critical of her "trivial" concern. However, when I mentally sat myself at her desk, typing and handling all the issues that came her way, I immediately experienced the same frustration about the table she had described. My

*Each person is an island unto himself, in a very real
sense; and he can only build bridges to other islands if
he is first of all willing to be himself and permitted
to be himself. . . . It is a very paradoxical thing—that
to the degree that each one of us is willing to be himself,
then he finds not only himself changing; but he
finds that other people to whom he relates are also
changing.*

Carl Rogers[46]

empathic state led me to suggest a solution I would never
have dreamed of while sitting in judgement of her.

4. Had Jake the courage to witness, own, and fully experience
    his reactions to his boss's response, his insight—or just his
    awareness—might have healed the breach.

    I once worked for a man who "pushed my buttons" in
    a way that seriously undermined my effectiveness. He called
    my favorite communication mode "philosophizing" and sum-
    marily dismissed most of what I had to say. Prior to meeting
    him, I had invariably been complimented on my communica-
    tion, so his response was a shock. Furthermore, I couldn't speak
    with him without feeling confused and incompetent. My first
    reaction, of course, was to mentally criticize him for his "rigid
    ways, linear thinking, and almost continual reference to what
    was 'proper.'"

    However, I took my own advice and focused my attention
    on witnessing my thoughts and feelings. One day, in his office,
    as I was noticing my uncharacteristic anxiety and lack of crea-
    tivity, it occurred to me (Aha!) to ask myself how old I felt in
    the presence of my boss. My intuitive answer came quickly, "9
    years old." I felt as confused and helpless as I often did then.
    From that point on, I stayed with that awareness (in a time-
    sharing way) whenever I was with my boss. After a period of
    time, I noticed that my 9-year-old state had faded away. We were
    subsequently able to resolve our communication differences
    and developed a warmly compatible working relationship.

    He is, to this day, one of my favorite people to work with.
    I had resolved all of our differences within myself.

5. Jake could have responded by beginning to keep track of his reactions. He could have started a journal wherein he noted precisely what pushed his button and his reactions each time— a written form of witnessing and an ancient and powerful technique. By keeping his journal and noting button-pushing patterns, he could sometimes function as his own therapeutic friend and thereby free himself.

6. Jake could find a therapeutic friend, perhaps a psychotherapist, minister or skilled acquaintance, to help him discover the source of his reaction.

7. Jake could try all of the above, and more. . . .

The main point of this discussion is that Jake does not allow himself to play the victim or to gunnysack. Instead, he courageously decides to "burn and learn." He looks within and outwardly, recognizing that his responses are the determining factors in his world. He knows that his boss can't make him feel frightened, angry, or depressed; he does that to himself. He realizes that his negative response signals opportunity for growth. Instead of merely reacting, he looks for the big payoff—his own freedom and competence—by witnessing and questioning himself. By doing so, he not only circumvents conflict appropriately, he grows toward his own powerful potential.

> *If you measure success in terms of praise and criticism, your anxiety will be endless.*
> *Having a good reputation or becoming well-known for your work can be a hindrance to your further development.*
> *Fame is as burdensome as caring for yourself properly.*
> *What is the problem with praise and criticism? If the group applauds one thing you do, and then you feel good, you will worry if they do not applaud as loudly the next time. If they are critical, if they argue or complain, you will feel hurt. Either way, you are anxious and dependent.*
> *How can a good reputation be a hindrance? A good reputation naturally arises from doing good work. But if you try to chrish your reputation, if you try to preserve it, you lose the freedom and honesty necessary for further development.*

On Disclosing Oneself

The healthier person will doubtless experience many a bruise for being and disclosing who he is, but he prefers to accept these blows rather than lose himself or sell himself (his authentic being) for short-run acceptability.

Sidney Jourard[22]

How is fame like caring for yourself? In order to do good work you must take good care of yourself. You must value yourself and allow others to value you also. But if you make too much of yourself, you will become egocentric. Egocentricity injures both self and work.

If you can live with the fruits of success and care for yourself properly, you will be able to foster success in other people.

John Heider[13]

Unfortunately, most people in Jake's shoes would not look within themselves in response to their feelings. Their ego-mind would react with reasons for the boss's behavior and angrily find a way to blame him or her. An alternate response (the other side of the same coin) would be to succumb to a sense of being incompetent. Either response is likely to lead to the erection of a Wall.

If the Wall went up between Jake and his boss and Jake decided this crisis was painful enough (perhaps because it jeopardized his career) to warrant seeking assistance, he may come to a facilitator like myself. Events would then likely follow a predictable pattern.

Jake will talk at great length and in vivid detail about how his boss has wronged him. He is likely to speak of being put down, perhaps even betrayed. He will tell me with great certainty just why his boss is acting this way. Jake's story will be complete in every detail, with nary a loophole. Further, he may ask me to contact others, say, Charlie, Mary, and Susan, who will verify that he is totally right.

Later, if they both agree to meet with me, the boss, Tina, will come and tell me about Jake. She will paint a vivid, complete, and unassailable picture of Jake, how he is wrong and why. She may tell me to contact Bill, José, and Dana who will prove she is right. She may even name the same people Jake did. Both Jake's and Tina's stories, their respective versions of reality, will appear perfectly logical and reasonable. Each apparently has commiserators to back up their respective views.

Neither of their visions of reality will prove to be accurate; each will turn out to be substantially a blind fabrication, the ego-mind's creation. When we meet for our conflict resolution session, the actual problem will prove to be significantly different than either Jake's or Tina's version.

It is often sadly obvious to me that people who come to me for conflict resolution assistance are creating their own problems, but they rarely will even consider this possibility. Ego is firmly in control. (Fortunately, this situation appears to be changing. More and more people have some experience with personal growth, often in connection with getting through a divorce or other major crisis.) Even with professional assistance, people deal with their difficulties by working out ways of being and working together without hurting each other (i.e., without pinching or pushing buttons). Ego thereby remains largely intact and in command, and each person remains vulnerable.

The fact is—and we must discover this for ourselves for it to be a fact—we each must give the power to hurt to the other. I give you the power by being vulnerable. I am tender and hurtable because, deep down, I don't love me. If I truly love and accept myself as I am, then you simply can't hurt me psychologically. And, when I truly love me, I can't help loving you and everyone else. That's how we come to love our neighbors as ourselves.

We come to love ourselves by finding ourselves. That's how it works.

> *The remarkable thing is that we really love our neighbor as ourselves; we do unto others as we do unto ourselves. We hate others when we hate ourselves. We are tolerant toward others when we tolerate ourselves.*
> *Eric Hoffer*

Moral: By waking up to the witness in
ourselves and noting our responses
to those who irritate or upset
us, we develop options for dealing
with conflict that are more
powerful and permanent than
confrontation. Our willingness to
face ourselves rather than merely
the others in our drama brings
growth toward our full personal
and professional potentials.

Finding One's Deeper Self

In order that a man be capable of straightening himself out, he must find his way from the casual, accessory elements of his existence to his own self; he must find his own self, not the trivial ego of the egotistic individual, but the deeper self of the person living in a relationship to the world.

Martin Buber[5]

15

C H A P T E R

SOME COMMON SOURCES OF CONFLICT

To disagree with anyone or anything is to run the risk of taking oneself out of the money. All this in a country that was born of controversy—a country that wrote controversy into its Constitution, and set up its legislative bodies on the theory of controversy, that established its free press in the belief that controversy is vital to information, and that created a system of justice of which controversy is the heart and soul.

E. B. White

Trying to write exhaustively about the causes of conflict would be like trying to describe every person in the world. We each must wake up to our own. Nevertheless, in the hope of helping to trigger your process of discovery, I will comment on some that I recall dealing with many times during the past 20 years. Ego-mind is at the bottom of each.

Making Others Wrong

If I were to offer the closest thing to a rule for getting along with others, I would say, "Don't make them wrong." Because of the ego, making another wrong or criticizing is the most common pinch, button push, or stone of all; the Wall will begin to go up immediately. I hasten to add that it is possible to avoid doing so without being a "wimp." Not making others wrong reflects an attitude that stems from recognizing that (a) most people want to do the right thing, (b) people are making the best choices from their own perspective, (c) most issues worth dealing with are too

*I have found that the more I can be genuine in
relationships, the more helpful it will be. This means
that I need to be aware of my own feelings, in so
far as possible, rather than presenting an outward
facade of one attitude, while actually holding another
attitude at a deeper or unconscious level.*

Carl Rogers[46]

complex to merit simple right vs. wrong distinctions, and (d) we all have
egos. So, we listen empathically for the merits of their points of view.
If we can't identify the merits, we ask about them. If we disagree, we
can acknowledge the merits and own our disagreement: "That's not the
way I see the situation."

An elegant way of dealing with our disagreements is to formulate
them as wishes or wonders: "I can see that your proposal makes sense
in this way and wonder what . . ." or "I wish I could think of what to do
when. . . ."

The usual and common practice of making others wrong almost
invariably evokes a defensive response and a desire for retribution—seeds
of conflict. Such reactions are, incidentally, a prime source of *committee*
rather than *creative* behavior in groups. When Harry offers up an idea,
other members of the group quickly tell him what's wrong with it; most
Harrys shut up, feel rejected, and wait their turn to shoot down someone
else's brainstorm. Creativity is hard to grow in such an environment.

Writing Memos

My second quasi-rule is, if at all possible, to avoid writing memos
or letters about potentially divisive issues. Recall that most communication
is approximately 95 percent nonverbal. A written message, therefore, is
relying upon the verbal 5 percent. Words have no objective meaning (recall
in Chapter 3 when Maria asked Jill if she enjoyed teamwork) so their meaning and the other 95 percent of the communication are supplied by the
recipient's mind! The probability of being accurately understood is minimal.

Furthermore, my experience in conflict resolution suggests that,
almost always, the provocative memo becomes a Wall in itself. People, particularly rational and analytical types, tend to treat the words on paper

as if they were written in stone by God. "What I meant was this." "Yes, but what you said was that!" Unfortunately, few people seem to realize that words are just strings of sounds to which we apply meanings.

Face-to-face is best by far for confronting effectively. The telephone is a distant second best. The written word often adds to the conflict.

Our Two Masters on the Job

Our work can be a source of fulfillment, a way of contributing to others, a way of expressing our gifts in the world, or a source of frustration and even fear. This recognition is so fundamental that one of the classic responses of the Zen Master to the student who asks how to determine progress in sitting meditation is, "How's your work going?" As we escape the domination of ego-mind, our work becomes easier and our effectiveness increases.

It has been said that one cannot serve two masters. Yet, each of us comes to our place of work with, in effect, two masters. One is the boss and the organization. The other—usually much more dominating and harder to satisfy—is ego. We have two competing agendas: one is to satisfy the demands of our egos and, at least nominally, to get the job done.

We can't do both at once. When we are concerned about our status, about getting enough recognition, about the size of our office, or about any of the other ego-motivated desires that we accept as normal, these concerns absorb energy. This energy is not available for the job.

Are you truly working for your organization? Or are you working for your ego? If you want recognition, strokes, a scientific reputation, power over others, to be "on top," to be called "Doctor," to live in the posh part of town, to win, to be admired, you are bound by your ego. Whether or not other motivations are influencing you, ego has a firm grip on your steering wheel. As I mentioned, we can't do two things at the same time and energy is limited. When we are working to satisfy our ego (and we *never* will succeed in doing so), some of our energy is not available for other possibilities.

The freer we are from ego-mind, the more effective we become. We may not realize it at first because our work seems so much easier as we lose our stressfulness and stop straining. What used to be very difficult now seems to fall into place. Solutions to problems somehow appear when we need them. We worry less about end results and what "they" will think, and so devote less energy to defending ourselves and more to doing a good job.

What the Zen Master knows is that sitting in meditation gradually quiets the mind. As our minds quiet or as we are able to witness our mental

On Map-Making

Our view of reality is like a map with which to negotiate the terrain of life. If the map is true and accurate, we will generally know where we are, and if we have decided where we want to go, we will generally know how to get there. If the map is false and inaccurate, we generally will be lost.

M. Scott Peck[44]

---

activity without being caught up in it, our concentration increases and we become focused on whatever we're doing. When we are one with what we are doing—typing, calculating, researching, or brick laying—we are in the here and now: this is meditation. We feel mellow and experience a clear, peaceful excitement. At these times, we are doing the best job we can possibly do.

Ego-mind is probably the greatest source of organizational inefficiency and conflict. You know how it works. Suppose Sam is perfectly content with his pay. Then he finds out that Carol, who has worked for the company just a short time and who is unquestionably less productive than him, makes more money. He crashes. Sam's ego has compared him with Carol and has lost. Anger, frustration, and depression follow. Outrage at the "unfairness" of his boss and/or the company spews from him. Nothing has changed but his awareness of Carol's higher salary, yet that's enough to send him into a tailspin. The house of cards that is his self-confidence or self-image has collapsed in the slight breeze of his knowledge of Carol's salary. Passive aggressiveness and/or overt conflict is likely to follow as a result of Sam's thoughts. (If Sam's ego were not in charge, the new information—Carol's salary—might lead him to a calm exploration of his "market value" and a discussion with his boss.)

We are stuck with two masters because we refuse to face the worst of them within ourselves.

I once had a client who was a top-flight scientist, a manager of many other scientists, who learned that members of the legal staff in his organization had new carpeting in their offices. This discovery seriously upset him. He launched a campaign to get his office carpeted which, for months, dominated his organizational existence and left him little energy for his professional work.

Of course, few of us—certainly not a rational, senior-level scientist and manager—would admit to having our egos crushed, our feelings hurt, in such a circumstance. Most people won't even admit such a thing to

Map-Making Requires Effort

We are not born with maps; we have to make them, and the making requires effort. The more effort we make to appreciate and perceive reality, the larger and more accurate our maps will be. But many do not want to make this effort....Their maps are small and sketchy, their views of the world narrow and misleading.
M. Scott Peck[44]

themselves, much less to their managers or to others. We have learned to glibly and readily rationalize in such situations. My client argued for rugs for his office "so that customers would be properly impressed," "so that the office would be quieter, hence more efficient," "so that the scientists who report to me would feel of equal status to the lawyers and not be demotivated," and the like. His boss (who easily saw through his rationalizations) finally tired of the arguments and had my client's office carpeted. I've sometimes wondered what would have happened then had the lawyers gotten, say, fancier desks.

The ego is the real enemy, if we have an enemy. We can easily see it in others. Our challenge is to find the courage to look within ourselves and watch our own ego in action. Chances are it's running us and keeping us in chains like no outside event or person ever could. Again, don't fight it or try to control it. Just look.

We are caught in ego's trap and in the mind's dramas and illusions because we don't pay attention to what's really going on within ourselves. (Sometimes we can't catch on to what's going on even when we do observe. That's where a good teacher, therapeutic friend, or therapist can make all the difference.) We are sleepwalking, unaware of what's happening—and it is awakening that gives us choice and control and sets us free.

Since internal discoveries usually come via Ahas that occur unexpectedly, in their own time, they can only indicate the process whereby witnessing is freeing. There is no way of formulating it, of writing a prescription for action. A very simple example involving external events may help explain. Years ago, in an organization I worked for, an ambitious middle manager spoke to a group of our top executives on a subject of considerable importance to them all. He spoke for about an hour, standing on a stage in front of the group. After he finished, a friend of his kindly informed him that, for the duration of his talk, his fly had been open. The experience was so traumatic for this man—so "hard on his ego"—that he developed a new habit, the effect of which was worse than leaving his fly open.

He began, unconsciously and periodically, to check his fly while speaking. The action was obvious to everyone but himself. Again, his friends came to his aid with feedback on his behavior. They provided, in effect, a mirror wherein he could see his own reflection (Aha!). Although he was disgusted with himself for his behavior, he was simultaneously freed of his blindness. (Often, at the moment of awakening, we can see something of how we kept ourselves asleep as we hear ego's judgement condemning what we find.)

Actually, the feedback did not immediately free him of his new habit of checking himself. What he gained from the feedback was the knowledge of what to witness/watch for. At first, he became aware of his checking only after he had checked, perhaps an instant later. However, as he paid attention to himself (and this is the way it usually works) the time that elapsed between his action and his awareness of his action gradually shortened. When he finally became aware of his action at the moment he was about to perform it, he was at last able to choose whether or not to check. When we are fully awake to our thoughts, feelings, and behaviors *as they occur*, our awareness automatically gives us control. That, at least on a behavioral level, indicates how the simple process of witnessing gradually produces such powerful and beneficial changes in our lives. (Again, please note that this is watching, not judging. When "the judge" in you gives you a hard time, notice that too.)

Our *real time awareness* enables us to manage ourselves. Once we are fully awake to what we are thinking or doing *as the thought or action happens*, we automatically have control and choice. We don't have to do anything except watch. We don't have to force anything or reprogram ourselves. We just gradually wake up to what's going on in us *now* and we can live as we choose. And, if we're in touch with the wisdom within ourselves, beyond ego and mind, we'll know what choice to make. Like not checking my fly in front of an audience. Along the way to full awakening to any patterns of action, we may notice them only after they have occurred. That's fine; keep on watching. Eventually, you'll be awake as it happens and you'll be free of it. It's very much like waking from a dream.

> It is far more important that one's life
> should be perceived than that it should
> be transformed; for no sooner has it
> been perceived, than it transforms itself
> of its own accord.
>
> *Maurice Mæterlinck*

The organization is a great place to witness egos and minds in action. We can use our daily work life as a kind of private university of ourselves. We will thereby also gain effectiveness (and, paradoxically, we may even be more likely to achieve some of the rewards our egos ache for).

One concern is likely to arise for some readers. People attending my seminars often recognize that ego is the chief motivator in their work culture and express concern that everything would come to a halt if we all got free of it. My first response is that I can't get very concerned because I don't expect ego to be eradicated during my lifetime. A more direct response is that ego is not the only motivator. Each of us has a life purpose that is revealed a bit at a time as we contact our real selves beyond the limits of ego-mind. Abe Maslow found it so when he did his classic and pioneering research on self-actualized people[31]. Contrary to his expectations, he found them in all walks of life. He found, for example, business people making lots of money for whom the money was a byproduct of doing what they loved to do. These people always win. They don't work or fight for ego. They don't work or fight for recognition, for external rewards, or for end results. The fact that they usually get them is secondary to the intrinsic rewards of responding to their inner calling. For such people, the process of doing their work is continuously rewarding, and because they are free of their egos, their lives are relatively free of conflict.

More On Ego

When we get down to basics, the fact is that our egos deplete our lives. Nothing else can take the credit. Even when working with sophisticated and relatively effective organizations, I sometimes feel I'm immersed in an ocean of egos, messing themselves up, blaming others for their problems and fighting. This is such a usual way of functioning that most people simply accept it. In fact, it's based on illusion: the majority of our conflicts are based on our own fantasies.

Most of us, for example, have had upsetting experiences in traffic. I was driving down the right lane of a four lane highway and overtook a car traveling well below the speed limit. I moved over to the center lane to pass. As I did, the other car sped up and attempted to keep me from returning to the right lane. I saw my turnoff up ahead and outran the other car in order to exit. As I managed to pull ahead, the young man driving the other car gave me an obscene gesture. I have, in the past, become very upset in such situations, and I've done some crazy driving to exact what revenge I could.

When I finally stepped back and witnessed what actually went on, I noted the following. The other driver sped up and blocked my way, then made his gesture. That's all; I did the rest. I had lots of choices of how to react. With little or no inconvenience, I could have slowed down,

*A life of total dedication to the truth also means a
life of willingness to be personally challenged. The
only way that we can be certain that our map of
reality is valid is to expose it to the criticism and
challenge of other map-makers. Otherwise we live
in a closed system—within a bell jar, to use Sylvia
Plath's analogy, rebreathing only our own fetid air,
more and more subject to delusion.*

M. Scott Peck[44]

even stopped by the side of the road for a moment. If I were feeling centered
and okay about myself, his finger would be just a finger and only he would
suffer (from his own anger). But if my ego is in control, I have to win the
race; ego can't let the other guy win or have his way. Also, my ego gets very
insulted by his gesture and burns to damage him in return.

Certainly, the guy in the other car was driving dangerously and
acting like a jerk (i.e., from his ego). Nonetheless, I don't have to take the
bait, and if I don't, the game is over. He has to seek another driver who will
play his destructive game. My basic problem here is me, not him. The real
source of my conflict is my own ego.

Consider another situation that most people would deem more serious, although not unusual. I have three friends who were fired from high-
level positions. (Generally, only effective people get fired from such positions;
quietly incompetent people who don't make waves merely get moved aside.)
Each of these men immediately got a top-level job in another firm. In fact,
two of the three took over presidential positions. Yet, in spite of such imme-
diate success, all three of them privately suffered for years from the trauma
of being fired. (Two of the three would have hurt even longer if they hadn't
sought psychotherapy.) Even today, the mention of the experience will bring
a wince from any of them. And, of course, they were angry.

What's going on here? A lot was said about the act of firing, how
it was done, who was right, and who betrayed whom in each case. Although
important, these are secondary issues. Each of my friends was hurt primarily because of his own vulnerability to rejection and because he had
failed in ego's eyes. Although the details of each person's reaction were
complex and individual, basically each suffered because he falsely identified
with his work role and based his sense of self-worth on his performance
in that role. His boss didn't hurt him; being fired didn't hurt him; his
own ego-centered vulnerability hurt him.

Maps Must Be Revised

*But the biggest problem of map-making is not that
we have to start from scratch, but that if our maps
are to be accurate we have to continually revise
them....The process of making revisions, particularly
major revisions, is painful, sometimes excruciatingly
painful. And herein lies the major source of many of
the ills of mankind.*

M. Scott Peck[44]

---

*He who knows others is learned; he who
knows himself is wise.*

Laotse (6th century B.C.)

Demotions also bring great pain, hence often conflict. Many organizations would like to be able to move people in and out of managerial jobs. Although such moves are usually a technical challenge to the individuals involved, the major problem is the loss of status. Ego again. Identification with ego is so pervasive that all organizations have, to some degree, a complex set of status indicators: size or location of office, presence or lack of carpet, style of desk, dress code, place on the organization chart, and so on. In company towns these indicators extend into the community in terms of housing, club memberships, and simply who talks to whom. This is energy-consuming and conflict-inducing stuff. It is deadly serious to ego, and deadening chains to everyone involved.

Let's consider another big issue: discrimination. Discrimination illustrates ego's rule and enslavement in a number of ways. First, discrimination stems directly from the mistaken identity we take on. If we didn't falsely identify ourselves with our bodies, minds, countries, possessions, positions, and personalities, what would there be to stereotype? What or who would there be to discriminate against? Who would there be to put down so ego could be "better than"? Without ego, there is, of course, no need or desire for ego trips. Further, without ego—without identity as black, white, male, female, young, old, president, or janitor—who is there to feel hurt? How can your discrimination hurt me if I feel fine about me? It can't.

Now, here comes the fuzzy line. Others can impede me in a number of ways, externally. They can become, or contribute to the creation of, a problem for me to solve—like getting a job, becoming a manager, getting a top salary, buying the house I want, or getting into the college of my

Dedication to Truth

Truth or reality is avoided when it is painful. We can revise our maps only when we have the discipline to overcome that pain. To have such discipline, we must be totally dedicated to truth. That is to say that we must always hold truth, as best we can determine it, to be more important, more vital to our self-interest, than our comfort.

                                                    M. Scott Peck[44]

---

choice. If I am a green person in a society dominated by purple egos, life could be very difficult. However, there is absolutely no way for the purple folks to make me not okay, to put me down, to make me inferior; only I can do this to myself (by accepting the purple's view of me).

> *No one can make me feel inferior*
> *without my consent.*
>   *Eleanor Roosevelt*

Making the purple people wrong and fighting them is merely the other side of my own vulnerability, the angry side of my fear. My basic problem remains my own false view of myself and the need for acceptance generated by that view. As I get clear, I may indeed choose to fight for my rights, however, I will no longer have to fight for my ego.

All this is simple. It is not easy.

Dependency

Relationships with other people bring most of us our greatest joy as well as our deepest frustration and sorrow. And, of course, our conflicts. This is so because most relationships are based on need and desire. Everyone looks for recognition and acceptance—for love. Ever notice what we sing about? We don't write songs about the joys of making money or the wonders of life as an engineer or corporate executive. We don't sing about the stock market or compose sweet poems to a computer. When our hearts are allowed into the act we sing, and when we sing we sing mostly of love. Our songs betray us. We sing mainly of the joys of love found and the agonies of love lost. Love acquired from another and love taken away by another.

People look for strokes from others, particularly when they are feeling down or insecure. Those people they want strokes from are looking to still others—perhaps even back at them—for strokes. This network of stroke-seeking goes on and on. It's like most of us are in a big lifeboat, scared and lost, and are reassuring each other. I gain confidence because you say I'm okay and you gain confidence because I say you're okay—and, in fact, we're both shaky and underconfident. We're looking where we were taught to look—in the wrong place.

The only true confidence you or I will ever acquire will come from within. That's the way it is. Notice how your confidence can vary from high to low, even though nothing much changes in your environment. You're going along fine and some chance remark or passing look, or nothing at all apparent, triggers a downturn. Later you recover and everything is okay again. What's changing is not the world, but your view of it. Notice that when you feel "on top of the world" you have little or no need for strokes, but when you are down you can't get enough of them. Lots of folks, for example, get very sexy when they're feeling needy. Others find an excuse to spend time with the boss, hoping for a bit of recognition. Your boss, under similar circumstances, does about the same with his or her boss, and so it goes.

Notice again, please, the times when the sense that all is well comes over us, if only for an instant. No need for strokes then, right? If we get them, fine; if not, fine. Ego-mind is resting and we aren't needy for status, recognition, compliments, reassurance, or other forms of love from outside of ourselves. When ego-mind takes over again, when here and now is lost, we fall for the cosmic joke again; we seek outside ourselves from others seeking outside of themselves for what isn't outside any of us. When we seem to find it, sooner or later it disappears like a snowflake in the palm of our hands.

In an old Sufi story, Nasrudin seeks under a streetlamp for a key he has dropped in the dark by his front door. When asked by a friend why he is searching for the key out there under the lamp rather than in the dark doorway, he answers, "Because it's light out here."

Many people wish for more romance in their lives. Romantic love is viewed by virtually everyone at one time or another as the most intense and important of all relationships. It's the subject of most of our songs. We can look there to remind ourselves of what really goes on, to some degree, in most human relationships. Consider Tom and Mary. Like the rest of us, each has a sense of inadequacy, a part of themselves that seems defective, unattractive or even totally missing. Let's say, in Mary's case, that she feels physically unattractive. She thinks she's too big here, too small there, and not quite right someplace else. Tom's "missing part" could be that he thinks he's not really smart or clever enough.

Tom and Mary meet and fall in love. In part, what that means is that Tom says, verbally and nonverbally, to Mary, "Gee, you're beautiful!" and Mary says to Tom, "You're smart!" Each thereby gets their missing piece from the other. For Tom and Mary, "I love you" means "I love how I feel about *me* when I'm with you" or "I love the reflection of me that I see in your eyes." Together, attached, each feels relatively whole and okay. Parting brings pain because the missing piece is torn away. If one leaves the other (perhaps because he or she found someone or something else that provided a better version of the missing piece), the ego of the rejected person adds to the pain by seeing in the rejection further verification of the imperfection. For example, if Tom leaves Mary for another woman, Mary "knows" it is because she is less attractive and therefore undesirable (and she may frantically enter into other relationships to ease her pain). Short of leaving, Tom's noticing other women can induce Mary's pain and thereby bring on conflict between them.

Another commonly "missing" element in people's lives is a parent. Like the old love song says, they want "someone to watch over me." Hardly anyone seems ready to take full responsibility for their lives, so what better approach (however unconscious it may be) than to find a substitute parent. This is certainly an underlying theme in many marriages. Somehow, she can spot her "Daddy" across a crowded dance floor on that "enchanted evening," and he spots his "Mommy." When the fit is good, they marry and take turns parenting each other and having childish tantrums. One of the most common words in our popular songs is "baby." He's my baby. She's my baby. You're my baby. He sings it to her and she to him. When I discuss this at my seminars, it gets a lot of knowing laughs. It is funny, except when it hurts.

One of my teachers calls romantic love "business." That's an accurate description. It's certainly more an exchange than "something made in heaven." Love, it ain't. For most of my life I thought it was. I grew up in Los Angeles and swallowed whole the old Hollywood version of life. I've strongly resisted waking up to this false and romantic view. It seemed like a big deal to give up. After all, if I could "marry an angel" like the old song said, I would certainly prove I (that is, ego-I) was a terrific guy and be taken care of to boot.

These are very simplified descriptions and real people are much more complex, but don't these descriptions basically fit?

The same essential process dominates the work scene. Most supervisors and managers seek out their positions at least partly to gain more status, more prestige—to fill in a missing sense of adequacy or self-worth. Of course, most nonmanagement employees also believe that they have similar missing pieces.

The workplace is also influenced by the archetypal parent-child nature of the organizational hierarchy. Simply speaking, the employee (as child) looks up to, defers to, obeys, pays attention to, and otherwise treats the manager as a very okay, if not superior, person. The manager, thereby, gets his or her missing piece filled in. The "good" manager (as parent) provides wise guidance, direction, supportive feedback, and rewards that fill in the nonmanager's missing sense of adequacy and security. Some organizational consultants believe that the Oedipus complex is often also a factor (more on this later). Neither party can afford to notice the other's feet of clay.

Each party in most relationships depends to some extent upon the other for his or her own feelings of self-worth. This is particularly true in close relationships. For example, for the husband to maintain a sense of confidence and well being, the wife must behave in a certain way: use the right words, have the right facial expressions, never refuse certain requests. Every child experiences this conditional love: if the child doesn't behave in a certain way at a certain time, Daddy gets very upset. Even distant relationships smack of such dependency. Most people get upset if a total stranger, perhaps a sales clerk, doesn't treat them politely.

If our happiness depends on another person's actions being just so, or if we can't stand them behaving in a particular way, then our relationship is essentially an addiction. Saying that we depend upon something, or someone, to keep us happy is the same as saying that we have an addiction. That's another way of looking at the real nature of most relationships. Chances are, all of ours include addiction. If we get upset when our boss or our kids or our spouse looks at us the "wrong" way or says the "wrong" thing, then we are addicted. And vulnerable. Ego is our master.

Although these descriptions are highly simplified, they do help steer us toward another key reason our relationships involve so much conflict: we want or "need" so much from others to feel okay about ourselves. When our needs are not met, we become upset, depressed, and angry with them. Unfortunately, psychology has reinforced this view by teaching us that it is "normal" to be so vulnerable. By and large, it certainly is, however, the true problem is not that our needs are not being met, it's that we have the needs in the first place! Our problem is our egos with their insatiable needs for reinforcement.

If, instead of working on ourselves, we attack the other person—or enter into conflict over what they have or have not done for us—we may indeed get results. We may get our "needs" met. Marriage counselors and OD practitioners facilitate such "solutions" all the time. However, such solutions are unlikely to be fully satisfactory or permanent because they are, like bandaids on a cancer, simply a cover-up for the real problem within.

The way out from under ego's yoke is to remember, again—and again and again and again—that our frustrations with others have nothing to do with anyone else. They have only to do with our desires, our needs, and our *reactions* to the other person, for which we are entirely responsible. Hence, we may gratefully regard people who expose our addictions, our vulnerabilities, our ego, as our teachers. We can thank them silently and, with courage, witness what's going on inside ourselves. We can stay with our pain and see where it comes from rather than lashing out, diverting our attention, or running away. We can do our best to discover our own patterns of behavior that contribute to the hurts we feel. Sometimes, if the pain or fear or anger is just too much to handle by ourselves, we may need a therapeutic friend who can help us to see ourselves and to stay with it until understanding emerges.

It's the same with all of us. True freedom, happiness, and peace come at a price, and the price sometimes involves staying with our own fear and pain long enough to get beyond our ego. We have to find the courage to do so again and again in our journey toward the peace that surpasses all understanding. Clarity and freedom come to us a bit at a time, not all at once. (One of ego's tricks may be to discourage you if you haven't gotten yourself all together by next weekend.)

As we find our way out of addiction, we become—or more accurately, find the space within ourselves where we are—detached, in the yogic sense of that term. In this sense, detachment means something like love without need or desire. Detachment comes with real love; a logical paradox, nevertheless, a fact. When I find the true love within me, I give freely and wisely without wanting anything in return and I allow others to be just as they are. True love has no object yet brings me close to all; it includes everyone and requires no one. It lies beyond all understanding and, when realized, is an everyday gift. This gift is a key to fulfilling relationships and true leadership in every walk of life.

> *Leaders are in love—in love with the*
> *people who do the work, with what*
> *their organizations produce, and with*
> *their customers....Leadership is an affair*
> *of the heart, not of the head.*
> *James M. Kouzes, Barry Z. Posner*[27]

The experience of this space of loving detachment seems all too rare in most of our lives. At best, it comes and goes, apparently of its own accord. The more in touch with reality we become, the more we get beyond ego and mind, the more likely it is to come and stay awhile. Between its visits, we can witness. We can notice that we have wants, that we get upset when other people don't give us what we want, and that what we crave is (usually) some form of stroking. We can note how often this will lead to conflict if we let it. We can observe this again and again. It takes alertness and courage. And it pays off, eventually, in self-confidence, in wisdom, in freedom, and in love from the only place they are truly available—within ourselves.

> *When one is a stranger to oneself, then*
> *one is estranged from others too.*
> Anne Morrow Lindbergh

Moral: The real heavies in our destructive conflicts are almost invariably our own egos (which our culture teaches us to promote rather than to subdue). The way to freedom from ego-mind's domination is the discovery or realization of the truth. As we wake up to who we are and how things actually work, we naturally become more effective. The price of our progress is seeing through the self-deceptions that dominate our existence and promote needless conflicts. As I wake up to being my own worst enemy I become my own best friend.

E P I L O G U E

We are free only so far as we
are not dupes of ourselves, our
pretexts, our instincts, our
temperament. We are freed by
energy and the critical spirit—
that is to say, by detachment
of soul, by self-government.
So that we are enslaved, but
susceptible of freedom; we are
bound, but capable of shaking
off our bonds.
                    Henri Frederic Amiel

Here is a wrap-up of the foregoing material, with emphasis on what each of us can do to manage the inevitable conflicts in our lives and to turn them from disagreeable disadvantages into steps toward deliverance.

Letting Go Of Pettiness

A man must die, that is, he must free himself from
a thousand petty attachments and identifications....
He is attached to everything in his life, attached to
his imagination, attached to his stupidity, attached
even to his sufferings, possibly to his sufferings more
than to anything else....Attachments to things, identifications with things, keep alive a thousand useless
I's in a man. These I's must die in order that the big
I may be born. But how can they be made to die?
They do not want to die. It is at this point that the
possibility of awakening comes to the rescue.

Gurdjieff[40]

WHAT TO DO

Reject your sense of the injury and the injury itself disappears.

Marcus Aurelius Antoninus (2nd century)

In many situations, whether on the job or in the family, the approach presented in Part II is invaluable. Managing conflict by confronting pinches effectively is crucial to our day-to-day effectiveness and well being.

In addition to developing conflict management skills, we can come to manage most conflicts (and our lives) in a joyful manner and at a level of competence undreamed of by most people. The key to doing so is our willingness to "burn and learn" and to find the sources within ourselves to eliminate and resolve conflicts without confronting others.

Burn and Learn

It may seem paradoxical that the very acts, attitudes, thoughts, and feelings that typically promote conflict can instead promote growth toward one's full potential. They are blessings-in-disguise. The work scene and, particularly, the home environment are crucibles of growth for most people. Both, as previously noted, are family or parent-child archetypes. At work, the organizational hierarchy places the manager in a strongly parental position as the provider of resources, direction, knowledge, judgement, rewards, and punishment. Even the terminology is loaded with triggers: "subordinates" are "junior" to "supervisors" or "superiors." The boss is in a position to direct and to judge performance, and to praise or criticize accordingly. He or she decides the salary level of, and can even unilaterally banish, an employee. Anyone in a "subordinate" position—and that's anyone below "Chairman of the Board"—can easily have his or her child response evoked.

The whole hierarchical setup triggers the child in people: feelings of anger, helplessness, inferiority, and the desire to be stroked and cared for. (Not exactly the dynamic traits most managers claim to want!) People who are childlike as subordinates—careful, obedient, unquestioningly loyal, and concerned more with what the boss wants than what the job needs—tend to become parental managers. (Another child response is rebellion, but since open rebellion gets people fired, it mostly shows up as inertia in the system.) Many (most?) organizations are rigid hierarchies wherein much energy is tied up by, in effect, children desperately working to get parental approval. It's not my intention to write a text on organizations; there are already too many. I want to emphasize that you can use the organizational arena for growth if you are willing to notice, with courage, your own responses. Any negative response, any button pushed, is an indicator of your incompleteness, of something you're not seeing in yourself. Blaming the boss, criticizing the organization, commiserating with coworkers, depressing yourself, complaining about your salary—particularly without taking full responsibility for your situation and without taking constructive (and perhaps risky) action to correct it—are indications that you are "in your child." It is the "not okay child"[16] aspect of the ego that wants and expects others to make everything right and curses them for not meeting its expectations.

In the example on page 106, as my child response to my boss faded, a new and highly effective working relationship developed between us; our differences blended us into a great team.

The Oedipus complex is another factor to watch for. Recently, I facilitated a conflict resolution meeting between a senior manager and a junior manager reporting to him. Several other participants in the conflict were also present. All were engineers or scientists. A very important and high-profit project was on the verge of failure because of the conflict. They had attempted, and failed, to find a solution.

My way of doing this kind of work is to rely on getting an Aha that tells me what the problem is. After working with them for a few hours it came. I realized that I was seeing the Oedipus complex in action. I shared my gestalt with the participants, pointing out that, basically, the Oedipus complex says that children often unconsciously form strong attachments to the parent of the opposite sex and want to displace the parent of the same sex. Males, in particular, become antagonistic toward their fathers.

When I pointed this out as a possibility, the faces of everyone in the room lit up. That was clearly what was going on. The younger manager saw it immediately. He (the son) was pushing and trying to get around his boss (the father) in every way possible and hadn't been able to see that. All along, the senior manager had been attempting to assist him in every way he could. We ended the meeting, by mutual consent, on this powerful note.

On Responsibility

Responsibility is the experience of being a determinant of what happens. Responsibility is the affirmation of one's being as the doer *in contrast to the acceptance of the role of the* object *done-to.*

J.F.T. Bugental[8]

The next afternoon they all dropped into my office to tell me that they'd gotten together earlier that morning and quickly solved their logistic and technical problems, thereby putting the project back on track.

The family environment is also a land of opportunity for personal growth (whether we like it or not). The family arena gives most people more opportunities to burn and learn than they can experience anywhere else. Not only is it an actual parent-child place, it is also an archetype of "home" for the adults, so it's easy to evoke their "child." At times, the family scene is dominated by unconscious craziness—by, in effect, kids (of all chronological ages) all wanting and competing for the center of the stage. Home is also, for most, the safest place to vent anger and to act out hostility—in other words, to let their fear loose. And at times, it can be literally a hell of a place. When it is and we want to grow, we won't run from the heat or blame it on others (or we'll at least witness ourselves doing so).

Adversity is the first path to Truth.
Byron

We remember that our reactions are our problems, that no one else is to blame for the way we feel or act. Instead of attempting to get others to change so we won't become upset (that's a losing battle anyway), we change ourselves so we're not so vulnerable. We do so by observing ourselves, not by forcing any change in ourselves. We observe what's going on in us, even if it's painful to do so (and it often is). As we get clear, we will automatically change. Nature is not perverse; we were not poorly designed; we have gotten lost and forgotten who we are. Self-remembering is the key to the doors of recognition. Consider the intensity at home to be a blessing in disguise, a gauge of your incompleteness, an opportunity to escape from the enslavement of your own image of self-importance. It does take guts. And persistence. By self-discovery I change in ways beneficial not only to me, but also to everyone else in my world. As I continue to face the tigers in myself, sometimes while holding hands with a thera-peutic friend for support, I gradually lose them.

As I have lost them, my faith in the process has grown stronger, so that now it's just a natural part of my life to pay attention to my inner, as well as outer, world. No end to my discoveries, my gradual metamor-phosis toward freedom. I just remembered the saying, "The price of liberty is eternal vigilance." We need to do our best to stay awake, to become as centered as we can.

When we are dominated by ego, when the child in us avoids respon-sibility and continually seeks external gratification, then we are far from centered. Stroke seeking—Recognition, status, reputation, power, fame. Attempting to be worthy in the eyes of others. Searching for someone who will magically make things right, the perfect parent. Searching for someone to fill the existential loneliness. Looking everywhere outside for the answer to "is this all there is?" All these are futile efforts to find what is already inside, misplaced like a pencil lost behind one's own ear.

All of these efforts to reduce anxiety produce anxiety, so the search becomes more frantic and more frustrating. It is only when we are centered, not thinking, and out from under ego's yoke that our anxiety goes. When we are centered, we don't have worries. The path to living is inward; diver-sions, distractions, and entertainments are only temporary hiding places.

An ancient and powerful method of personal growth is to isolate one's self away from all external stimuli, to go out into the desert alone or to lock one's self in a monastic cell, so that one has to hear and deal with all the fears and voices within. We don't need a desert or a cell. We have our work and home situations as vivid teachers or reminders of the job ahead. Next time, instead of lashing out, lay back, burn awhile, and discover what you are ready to discover. Somewhere along the way, you may be graced by also hearing the wee voice of wisdom within you, letting you know your next step and reminding you that, actually, all's well.

Resolve Conflicts Without Confronting Others

Finally, one of the extraordinary benefits of the witnessing and awakening process is the resolution of conflicts without arguing with any-one. In addition to the previous examples, an example from my own life is particularly vivid. My youngest son, Rich, was 17 and a master at pushing my buttons. He could annoy me no matter how much I watched myself. Rich, my wife Marlys, and I were driving to the coast. On the way, we stopped overnight in a motel. The day was hot, and although I was just

Where to Begin

The essential thing is to begin with oneself, and at this moment a man has nothing in the world to care about other than this beginning. Any other attitude would distract him from what he is about to begin, weaken his initiative and thus frustrate the entire bold undertaking.

Martin Buber[5]

recovering from the flu, I had worn shorts and sandals for the trip. Rich had engaged in some button-pushing during the trip, and by the time we arrived at the motel I was already somewhat irritated.

After we checked in, we parked outside our room. Rich grabbed the key and took off for the room, leaving us to carry the luggage *(push)*. Marlys and I loaded ourselves with suitcases and walked toward the main entry. We had to pass by the sliding glass doors opening from our room onto a strip of shrubbery and lawn where the sprinklers were running. As we passed, Rich opened the doors and urged us to walk through the sprinklers directly into the room. Marlys hurriedly did so. I replied that I didn't want the cold water on my bare legs and feet, and that I would go around to the inside door. Rich agreed. I expected him to be waiting with the door open. However, when I got there it was closed and locked *(push!)*. I knocked. No response *(push!!)*. Again. No response (push!!!). By the time Rich opened the door I was very angry. He calmly and slowly opened the door *(push!!!)*. I charged into the room to find he'd turned on the radio full blast to a hard rock station *(push!!!)*. I started to rave at him and he just quietly looked at me and said something like, "Well, if you're going to act that way and ruin our trip, I'm sorry I came with you." *PUSH!!!* At that moment, Marlys entered the room to see Rich looking calm and me looking livid. She wanted to know what was the matter with me! I got control of myself, excused myself as being tired and asked them to go shopping while I took a nap. They did, and I lay on the bed reviewing what had just happened, particularly my responses and obvious buttons: I did some delayed witnessing.

Aha! The game hit me! The way it worked was that Rich would bait me with very subtle pushes. (They had to be subtle, just a slight remark or look, or there could be no payoff for him—namely, making Dad look like a big jerk. If the bait were obvious, the observers, usually Mom and his brothers, would consider him to be the problem, not Dad.) He would keep up his baiting, usually unconsciously, until I finally took the bait, then he would reel me in. I looked and felt like a big dunce—out of control, angry, and somehow guilty. In the situation I just described he continued pushing until I lost control and flew into a rage; he calmly collected his pay-off, in front of Mom, with me looking and apparently acting like a lunatic.

When Rich and Marlys returned to the motel, I shared my new discovery with them. Rich was, at first, very defensive and vigorously denied his role in the game. I persisted, genuinely complimenting him on his skill at hooking me. Gradually, a smile came over his face and he acknowledged, "Yes, I'm really good at it." We both laughed and hugged each other.

I now knew what to watch for, or so I thought, as we continued our trip to the coast on the following day. When he baited me I either silently watched my response or complimented him: "That was a good one, Rich, but you'll have to try again." We had a better time than usual. Nevertheless, just as we arrived at our seaside motel, he had me hooked again, this time by the way he drove the car. As I started to explode, Marlys said to me, "You let him get you again, didn't you?" I said, "Yes," thanked her, became fully awake to my reaction and let it go—another bit of freedom gained.

Something inside me kept saying that I was not seeing everything yet. I was still wondering, later that night, as I watched the moonlight play on the waves outside our window. Marlys was half asleep on the bed. I casually asked her, "There's something I'm not seeing and I don't know what it is, do you?" She responded by saying that I dealt with Rich in a different way than with anyone else, that I "gave myself away to him." Aha! I saw in a flash that it was so. I (that is, my ego) wanted him to love and admire me so much that I curried strokes from him and was easily hurt if his response was anything but positive. This behavior was, indeed, uncharacteristic of me (and virtually guaranteed a negative response from Rich, as it would from me if our positions had been reversed). This new awareness freed me completely from my vulnerability to Rich's baiting. Our trip home was free of stress because I was no longer reacted to the bait. Rich and I became significantly closer.

This example illustrates and reminds us of a number of important truths. First, when people are in conflict with each other, no one is at fault. *No one is to blame.* There's always a dance going on, each person's moves coordinated with the other's. The usual, and easy, response is to play the blame game. I could have done so with Rich, and believe me, in my anger I wanted to! I could easily have found other parents to commiserate with, to agree with me that Rich was "wrong" to bait his father as he did. My ego, of course, also wanted to make Rich wrong and tell him how to straighten himself out. I could have thereby made myself "right" and my ego would have loved it. The fact (as always) was that either of us could unilaterally end the conflict, Rich by stopping his baiting or me by not getting hooked.

We also could have resolved the conflict by making the problem clear and having Rich agree not to bait me anymore. While this approach could have worked to set aside the conflict, it would have left me with my vulnerability and Rich without the desire to face himself. It's an approach analogous to giving a person with a broken leg a crutch for life. It's also the way most people live, carefully surrounded with people who won't push their buttons, associating with people who agree with their views, and generally conspiring unconsciously to remain as they are. Fortunately, however, and paradoxically, nature arranges crises in our lives that make it difficult for us not to grow.

This example also illustrates that relationships can usually and elegantly be improved *unilaterally*. I didn't make Rich wrong or ask anything of him. On the contrary, I fully accepted him—forgave him in the full sense of the word.[17] I healed *myself*, and the love waiting under the surface emerged and did the rest. *Once I became fully aware of my actions, the solution was automatically there.* No mutual problem-solving or therapy was needed; my contacting reality set us free.

> *To understand is to forgive, even oneself.*
> *Alexander Chase*

Some of the truth, my first Aha, came as I witnessed myself. My second Aha came in connection with feedback from a therapeutic friend, in this instance my wife. As the great masters and sages have done for centuries, she held up a mirror so that I could see myself. As happens with insights, my seeing and doing happened simultaneously.

The incident I just shared happened years ago. Rich and I have never played that destructive game again. Nor has our closeness as father and son—and as dear friends—ever wavered. All because I got out of my own way.

Learning to manage conflict by effective confrontation is invaluable. For the individual, dissolving conflict in self-discovery is infinitely more so.

Moral: What to do, besides learning the skills described in Part I and confronting differences as they arise, is to confront ourselves—repeatedly, as often as necessary, until we are unencumbered by needless conflict and free to be all we can be.

A Great Treasure

There is something that can only be found in one place. It is a great treasure, which may be called the fulfillment of existence. The place where this treasure can be found is the place on which one stands.... Our treasure is hidden beneath the hearth of our own home.

Martin Buber[5]

BIBLIOGRAPHY

1. Alberti, Robert E., and Michael L. Emmons. *Your Perfect Right: A Guide to Assertive Living*, 5th edition. San Luis Obispo, California: Impact Publications, 1986.

2. Angyal, Andras. "A Theoretical Model of Personality Studies." *Journal of Personality*, September 1951, p. 47.

3. Assagioli, Roberto, M.D. *Psychosynthesis*. New York: Viking Press, 1965.

4. Bretall, Robert (ed.). *A Kierkegaard Anthology*. New York: Random House, 1946, p. 6.

5. Buber, Martin. *Hasidism and Modern Man*. New York: Harper and Row, 1966, pp. 156-159.

6. Buber, Martin. *Israel and the World: Essays in a Time of Crisis*. New York: Schocken Books, 1963, p. 42.

7. Buber, Martin. *The Knowledge of Man: Selected Essays*. Maurice Friedman, Editor and Translator. New York: Harper and Row, 1965, p. 69.

8. Bugental, J.F.T. *The Search for Authenticity: An Existential-Analytic Approach to Psychotherapy*. New York: Holt, Rinehart and Winston, 1965, pp. 23, 348-349.

9. Burns, David D. *Feeling Good*. New York: William Morrow, 1980.

10. Fordyce, Jack K., and Raymond Weil. *Managing with People*, 2nd edition. Reading, Massachusetts: Addison-Wesley Publishing Company, 1979.

11. Fromm, Erich. *The Revolution of Hope: Toward a Humanized Technology*. New York: Harper and Row, 1970, p. 110.

12. Hagberg, Janet O. *Real Power*. Minneapolis, Minnesota: Winston Press, 1984.

13. Heider, John. *The Tao of Leadership*. Atlanta, Georgia: Humanics New Age, 1985.

14. Hitt, William D. *The Leader-Manager*. Columbus, Ohio: Battelle Press, 1988.

15. Horney, Karen, M.D. *Neurosis and Human Growth*. New York: W. W. Norton, 1950.

16. James, Muriel, and Dorothy Jongeward. *Born to Win*. Reading, Massachusetts: Addison-Wesley Publishing Company, 1977.

17. Jampolsky, Gerald G. *Love Is Letting Go Of Fear*. Millbrae, California: Celestial Arts, 1979.

18. Jaspers, Karl. *The Future of Mankind*. Chicago: The University of Chicago Press, 1961, p. 227.

19. Jaspers, Karl. *General Psychopathology*. Chicago: The University of Chicago Press, 1963, pp. 326-327.

20. Jaspers, Karl. *Philosophy II*. Chicago: The University of Chicago Press, 1970, p. 54.

21. Jaspers, Karl. *Reason and Anti-Reason in Our Time*. New Haven: Yale University Press, 1952, p. 41.

22. Jourard, Sidney. *Disclosing Man to Himself*. New York: Van Nostrand Reinhold Company, 1968, pp. 47, 220.

23. Jourard, Sidney. *Healthy Personality: Approach from the Viewpoint of Humanistic Psychology*, 4th edition. New York: MacMillan, 1980, pp. 231, 238.

24. Kaufmann, Walter (ed.). *Basic Writings of Nietzsche*. New York: Random House, 1968, p. 451.

25. Kelen, Emery (ed.). *Hammerskjold: The Political Man*. New York: Funk and Wagnall Publishing Company, 1968, p. 41.

26. Knight, Margaret (ed.). *Humanist Anthology: From Confucius to Bertrand Russell*. London: Pemberton Publishing Company, 1967, p. 21.

27. Kouzes, James M., and Barry Z. Posner. *The Leadership Challenge*. San Francisco: Jossey-Bass, 1987.

28. Krishnamurti, J. *Freedom from the Known*. New York: Harper and Row, 1969, p. 58.

29. Maslow, Abraham. *Eupsychian Management*. Homewood, Illinois: Richard D. Irwin, 1965, pp. 162-163.

30. Maslow, Abraham. *The Farther Reaches of Human Nature*. New York: Viking Press, 1971, p. 34.

31. Maslow, Abraham. *Motivation and Personality*, 2nd edition. New York: Harper and Row, Second Edition, 1970.

32. Maslow, Abraham. "Synanon and Eupsychia." *Journal of Humanistic Psychology* 7, 1967.

33. Maslow, Abraham. *Toward a Psychology of Being*. New York: Van Nostrand Reinhold Company, 1968, p. 122.

34. Maslow, Bertha (ed.). *Abraham Maslow: A Memorial Volume*. Monterey, California: Brooks/Cole Publishing Company, 1972, p. 86.

35. May, Rollo. *Love and Will*. New York: W. W. Norton and Company, 1969, p. 146.

36. Mayer, R. J. "Keys to Effective Appraisal." *Management Review*, June 1980.

37. Mayer, R. J. "The Panacean Conspiracy." *Management Review*, June 1983.

38. Mayer, R. J. "The Secret Life of MBO." *Human Resource Management*, Fall 1978.

39. McKeon, Richard (ed.). *Introduction to Aristotle*. New York: Random House, 1947, p. 390.

40. Metzner, Ralph. *Opening to Inner Light*. Los Angeles: Jeremy P. Tarchner, Inc., 1986, pp. 37, 55, 146.

41. Mill, John Stuart. *On Liberty*. New York: The Bobbs-Merrill Company, 1956, pp. 44-45.

42. Moustakas, Clark. *Loneliness and Love*. Englewood Cliffs, New Jersey: Prentice-Hall, 1972, pp. 102-130.

43. Moustakas, Clark (ed.). *The Self: Explorations in Personal Growth*. New York: Harper and Row, 1956, p. 91.

44. Peck, M. Scott. *The Road Less Traveled*. New York: Simon and Schuster, 1978, pp. 44-45, 50-51, 52, 152.

45. Plato. *Philebus*. **In** Jowett, B. (ed.), *The Dialogues of Plato*. New York: Random House, 1920.

46. Rogers, Carl. *On Becoming a Person*. Boston: Houghton Mifflin Company, 1951, pp. 21-22, 33, 331-332.

47. Rogers, Carl, and F. J. Roethlisberger. "Barriers and Gateways to Communication." *Harvard Business Review*, July-August 1952.

48. Russell, Bertrand. *The Art of Philosophizing and Other Essays*. Totowa, New Jersey: Littlefield, Adams and Company, 1974, p. 25.

49. Russell, Bertrand. *Unpopular Essays*. New York: Simon and Schuster, 1950, p. 104.

50. Samuel, William. *The Child Within Us Lives!* Mountain Brook, Alabama: Mountain Brook Publications, 1986.

51. Satir, Virginia. *Conjoint Family Therapy*. Palo Alto, California: Science and Behavior Books, Inc., 1967, p. 89.

52. Steindl-Rast, Brother David. *Gratefulness, The Heart of Prayer*. New York: Paulist Press, 1984.

53. Tart, Charles T. *Waking Up: Overcoming the Obstacles to Human Potential*. New York: New Science Library/Shambala, 1986.

NAME INDEX